THOUGHTS FOR A LIFETIME
MEANINGFUL NUGGETS OF LIFE

THOUGHTS FOR A LIFETIME
MEANINGFUL NUGGETS OF LIFE

LOUISE PARENTE, PH.D., LCSW

APPRECIATION PUBLISHING

Appreciation Publishing

Appreciation Publishing
Flemington, NJ
drlouiseparentephd.com

Cover design by Nicole Visconti
Book design by Glenn Bossik

ISBN: 979-8-9899589-1-7
Library of Congress Control Number: 2025913749

Printed in the United States of America

Contents

Contents

Contents

DEDICATION

With deep love and appreciation, I dedicate this, my third book to John my husband, whose love, and support, in sickness and health, has guided me throughout our life together.

To our special sons, John Jr., Donald, and Steven and our 12 grandchildren. May you all remember that if you truly want something, visualize it and make it happen.

And to God for keeping me on his path. I have been blessed and touched in ways that cannot be expressed. To all of you, thanks.

TO MY READERS

With a skip in my heart and a tear in my eyes, I am so happy to present this book to my readers. This is my third book which has roots in the creation of Parting Is Such Sweet Sorrow, saying goodbye to an eating problem, and Changing your Relationship with Food Once and For all, the Ultimate Workbook.

Throughout life we are faced with and experience many ups and downs. Periodically thoughts permeated my mind, and I found myself wanting to elaborate on them, this led to the creation of this book Thoughts for a Lifetime: Meaningful nuggets of life. Approximately 21 years ago my husband was diagnosed with Parkinsons Disease. I know the writing of my books and these Thoughts for a Lifetime helped me to find peace and express myself, something I am so grateful for. This is something I would recommend to anyone who desires to do so. The thoughts presented in this book are emotional, educational, philosophical or however I felt at that time. I found that it reinforced my value in life and all it brings.

It is my sincere wish that you will find value reading these thoughts whenever you choose to. This process has added to the reality that "I have more appreciation than loss in my life". I wish the same for you.

INTRODUCTION

"God wove a web of loveliness, of flowers and trees and birds,
But made not anything at all so beautiful as words.
They shine around our simple earth with golden shadowings.
And every common thing they touch is exquisite with wings."
　　　　　　　　—Anna Hempstead Branch

What follows is a compilation of my Thoughts for a Lifetime. Over the course of many years when I felt inspired by a thought, a word, a picture, or a feeling, I would write something that I titled Thoughts for a Lifetime. The act of writing and the use of words served as a form of expression I chose to explore.

The themes depicted in these Thoughts for a Lifetime are many. Some include information that I hope you will find helpful. Some focus on holidays, family, interpersonal relationships, food issues, as well as emotional and psychological factors. The creation of these helped me to understand many feelings both positive and negative. The need to feel and act with positivity, love, wisdom and knowledge will hopefully enlighten the reader.

This book is divided into four seasons. Each Thoughts for a Lifetime section does not follow an ongoing sequence, timeline, occasion or theme, they are varied and were randomly written. I have chosen to include the four seasons to introduce each section. To me, this represents the Seasons of Life. I believe that each section prepares us for the next. How we embrace them becomes the wind beneath our wings.

Throughout life we may encounter various challenges, some are associated with different stages also known as the Seasons of Life. We gain perspective, become more flexible and hopefully develop a more positive inner self that values purpose, love, kindness and understanding.

It is my sincere wish that the reader will find the following Thoughts for a Lifetime to be valuable in someway, at any time.

Spring - is associated with new beginnings, rebirth, renewal, hope and growth.
Summer – is associated with abundance, growth, rehabilitation, joy, passion and fullness of life.

Autumn – is associated with transition, and change, maturity and reflection.

Winter – is associated with rest, dormancy, reflection, peace and quiet strength.

Enjoy whenever, wherever and however you read the following.

Spring

New Beginnings · Renewal · Hope

ECCLESIASTES

Today I reflected on the words in The Book of Ecclesiastes.

To everything there is a season, and a time to every purpose under the heaven;

A time to be born and a time to die;
A time to plant and a time to pluck up that which is planted;
A time to kill and a time to heal,
A time to break down and a time to build up;
A time to weep, and a time to laugh;
A time to mourn and a time to dance,
A time to cast away stones, and a time to gather stones together;
A time to embrace, and a time to refrain from embracing;
A time to get, and a time to lose; a time to keep, and a time to cast away;
A time to rend, and a time to sew;
A time to keep silence, and a time to speak;
A time to love, and a time to hate;
A time of war, and a time of peace."
—1611 King James Version-translation

This beautiful passage reflects the ebb and flow of life, acknowledging that each season has its purpose and significance. It reminds us that change is inevitable, and there is wisdom in recognizing the right time for different actions and emotions.

It is placed here for no political or religious intent, other than something I thought about and wanted to share.

Many years ago a package was delivered to my home. In it was a mini white colored bible with the above words, until today I never found out why it was in this package. At the same time, I was applying to New York University's School of Social Work to study for a Master's in Social Work. As part of the application, I needed to write a biography. This passage was so appropriate for me, I used it as another reason why I was applying to this school at the time of life I was in. Yes, I was accepted and went on many years later to study for a PhD in Clinical Social Work there as well.

This saying was more than comforting and one that is always in my mind. It has been one that I call upon whenever I feel the need.

I hope you find the above as comforting as I do.

JOY

"Sometimes your joy is the source of your—smile, But sometimes your smile can be the source of your joy."
                                                        —Thich Nhat Hanh

In today's world we see and experience tragedies and joy. Are your eyes open to the joy that does surround us? There is the popular phrase, "Stop and Smell the Roses". It represents the importance of staying focused on something, not multitasking, or running somewhere else. I think it can mean many things to different people. Do you focus on your senses of smell, sight, taste, the ability to hear and touch? Do you allow yourself to Stop, Look, Listen and Feel?

Today please focus on JOY. What is your experience when you see a flower bloom or a newborn baby, when you make the college of your choice, get that special job, move to a new home, or maybe meet the guy or gal of your dreams? No matter what it is, stay in the moment to find JOY in it.

Today we MUST stay focused on what is positive, JOY is just that. Begin to create and see the good in things, not just the negative. Begin to see the positive and the contribution that it has on life. Joy is powerful. You will find people who want to join you on the journey of JOY. They will emulate your positive energy. Focus on it, it is within you. Become a leader of JOY.

Here goes!!!

Today, ask yourself, what is your joy? Live It! Enjoy it! Use it!

MY BOOKMARK

"A thing of beauty is a joy forever. It's loveliness increases. It can never pass into nothingness."

—Keats

Last week my granddaughter gave me a bookmark. It was newly crafted by a bookmark designer. Not only was I touched by this, but its significance added to another level of appreciation for her thoughtfulness. She followed my writing journey in which I authored and published two books. Her acknowledgment and sensitivity added to my joy. To me my bookmark represents beauty. This gift whetted my appetite to know more about "bookmarks" thus leading to this Thoughts for a Lifetime.

A bookmark is a practical tool to keep track of a reader's progress in a book. Historically bookmarks were used since the 1st Century AD, in fact the original was found near Sakkara Egypt and was made of ornamental leather. History shows some were made of parchment strips, cards, fabrics, metals, silk and much more. Collectable bookmarks emerged in the 1850's in England. They remain today and continue to serve as companions for book lovers that guide the reader through their literary journeys.

I found it interesting that in many cultures, they symbolize wisdom, knowledge and enlightenment. Personally, I prefer to read a physical copy of a book, thus my bookmark will continue to remind me of my connection to the printed words, history and my granddaughter.

My bookmark gift will be treasured each and every time I use it. Thank you, LLP!

IN MEMORY OF W.

"The only way to have a friend is to be one."
—Emerson

As I sit here to write today's Thoughts for a Lifetime, tears of sorrow trickle down my face.

News of the sudden, unexpected and unbelievable death of a special friend, someone who was like family and in our lives since childhood has reawakened the importance of life.

Being in life with loved ones we cherish is one of the greatest gifts we can give to each other.

My intention is not to delve into the stages of loss and grief, but rather to acknowledge how loss can affect the various aspects of our life. It is important to acknowledge the deep bond shared and recognize that healing is not a linear process.

It is my hope that this Thoughts for a Lifetime describes some aspects of the loss of special people and a reminder to recall the moments of connection and memories thus keeping the spirit alive. Do you agree?

"There is a destiny that makes us brothers. None goes his way alone. All that we send into the lives of others come back into our own."
—Markham

CONNECTION AND COMMITMENT

Today I woke up thinking about connection and commitment. Multiple thoughts, feelings and definitions whirled in my mind. Questions like, is there interrelatedness between connection and commitment, if so, what is it? Can one commit to something or someone and feel little to no connection? Some of my views on commitment and connection are as follows:

Connection

What is my experience? When I am connected to others I am in the moment, instead of thinking what I must do or what I want to do, this is a time to share.

I am "me", authentic and honest, expressing both my fears and joys. I feel a sense of trust.

My connection can be experienced in a conversation, making eye contact even with a passerby, or feeling grateful for others. My feeling of connection can be emotional, honest and realistic.

Commitment

Commitment influences development. If I dedicate myself to growth, I will continue to develop. Commitment requires action, persistence, dedication and consistency to affect my goals. This can relate to my personal or professional goals; it represents the basis of my "Human Connection" as I prefer to define it. It allows me to experience the importance of adaptability and identity. Both connection and commitment have multiple threads that tie them together. They both play essential roles in relationships; they shape depth and longevity.

Each one of us views things in their own way but in my mind, there is a CONNECTION between connection and commitment, they are part of who we are.

Let's not forget: Marie Curie, whose work on radiation phenomena, had its impact in the field of science. Her commitment to her work led her to be the 1st women to receive the Nobel Prize.

Nelson Mandela who endured 27 years of imprisonment due to his activism against the apartheid regime.

Helen Keller showed us that in her refusal to be defined by her disabilities, she became an influencer who has inspired us.

One of my commitments in writing Thoughts for Lifetime is to connect with you, the readers. And to ask you to take this belief further. What do you believe and how is connection and commitment represented in your definition of Life?

Thank you for your thoughts!

"Commitment is what transforms a promise into a reality."
—Abraham Lincoln

MOTHER'S DAY, 2023

"The love of a mother is the veil of a soft light between the heart and the heavenly Father."
—Samuel Taylor Coleridge

Today I walked outside and felt a light breeze, along with the sun starting to peak through a few clouds. The fragrance of the morning dew along with the budding blossoms added a sense of calm for me. These represented youth, beauty, and pleasure to me. Within a few minutes a family of deer were in my view, a total of four were grazing and communicating, in the way that deer communicate. There were two fawns who didn't move too far from their mother. The grace and beauty I was experiencing cannot be explained. It was the nature of their connection that touched me. All the above represented health, beauty, and vigor.

This was especially meaningful, for you see today is Mother's Day. I was touched, a feeling of gratitude and love was remembered. I was flooded by so many special moments I had spent with my mother before she passed. This and my own experiences with motherhood, the value, love, and connection rapidly surfaced. Mothers are part of our being, you may be a mother, if not, you had a mother (or mother figure). As you read this Thoughts for a Lifetime, perhaps acknowledgment and appreciation of mothers in life will brighten and lift you.

Today, let us look at the positive representation of mothers in our life; may we look at the positive in our life in ways that escape us.

"Mothers is the name for God in the lips and hearts of little children."
—William Makepeace Thackeray
(d. 1863)

LOVE

Dost thou love life? Then do not squander time, for that is the stuff life is made of."
—Franklin

Love and the ability to love is one of life's gifts which is to be accepted and treasured. Life can take on many forms. In life one can love their special people, family, friends, work, values, beliefs, the list goes on. When you love what you do, you excel, you feel motivated, gratified and special in so many ways.

To love is positive, it is not always without question, concern, and sometimes doubt. It sometimes tests our sense of inner thoughts and experiences.

In today's world there is so much love and commitment, yet we also experience doubt, differences in opinions and negativity; they are abounded. To think with an open mind can be extremely necessary and helpful.

Today, my purpose is to suggest that you allow yourself to feel, experience, learn and hold on, without exception, to your values. This will lead to self-acceptance and self- love and something that becomes infectious for those who you share it with.

"Where there is love there is life."
—Mahatma Gandhi

FREEDOM PLUS

Here it is Memorial Day Weekend, a time to give thanks to all who have served our country. It also begins with outdoor picnics, food, family & friends and fun. FOOD, DRINK, etc., can you enjoy it without it being a negative or unhealthy activity? Again, the question is do you know you have a negative relationship with it that has existed for years? Is negativity a result of life events? Do you think that you make a positive change in this area without acknowledging and experiencing the loss that comes with it?

I ask you to ponder the following regarding this subject:

1. Do you really want to change this relationship?
2. Are you ready to accept the fact that you want to change it?
3. If not, start a self-dialog to understand the inner conflicts that are active.
4. If you do not want to change it or have self-doubts, ask yourself:
   a. What you will be losing if you do not?
   b. What will you be losing if you do?

Each day take as much time that is needed to Stop, Look and Listen and Feel. Think about what was, what is and what will be. Your perseverance and intentions will follow.

In the above Thoughts for a Lifetime and others addressing this theme, please replace it with changing other negative relationships such as with alcohol, gambling, partners, compulsive shopping etc you may be plagued with.

BUNDLE OF QUOTES #1

BE BY EXAMPLE

Do you want to change the world And believe in its wonders? Start: By believing it can be.

By allowing it to be.
By protecting it.
By laughing more.
By getting up when you fall.
By appreciating that what comes into life is part of the journey.

To Be by Example means to believe in self. Believing in self leads to believing in the wonders of the world. BELIEVE IT AND BE IT BY EXAMPLE!

—Louise Parente

THE SOUL

The Soul is the seat of one's personality, will, intellect and emotions.
The Soul is the spiritual part of a human being and animal.
The Soul is part of a person which is not physical.
It experiences deep feelings and emotions.
The Soul is beyond special, Protect and Honor it.

—Louise Parente

START LIVING

It is never too late to change the way you think.
It is never too late to change a habit.
It is never too late to believe in and give hope.
It is never too late to live and let be.
It is never too late to start living.
So, begin to start living a life worth living.

—Louise Parente

13

TO WANT

"If you want to be happy, add sprinkles."
—Leo Tolstoy

Today's TFL focuses on "To Want". I was speaking to a friend about many things but the topic of what one wants got stirred up:

What do you want?
Is it okay to want?
Do you want to want?
Is it positive (good) or negative (bad) to want? The list goes on.

"To want" originally dates to around 1200 and meant "to be lacking". It has evolved to encompass both desire and need. I could delve into social inequity, its origins and explore the neuroscience of wanting and pleasure, rather I ask you to think about the following.

Everyone's experience, desire and belief of "to want" will most likely be diverse and very different. I strongly believe that both nature and nurture significantly shape our desires, wants and fears. Biological factors, genetic makeup, upbringing, environment, and culture add to our beliefs, emotions and conditioning: they are vital statistics in this quest.

I found myself wanting to understand "wants vs. needs". Yes, our needs are necessary for survival, security and health. But our wants go beyond the basic necessities, they include desires, preferences and the ability to enhance our quality of life.

I ask you to ponder this. My thought today is the importance of balance between the two. Life is a balance, to be aware of this, explore it and engage in the action it produces is where I "want" to be today and tomorrow. This is what I believe to be true. What do you believe?

"Until you do what you believe in, you don't know whether you believe it or not."
—Leo Tolstoy

ATTITUDE

"It is our attitude at the beginning of a difficult task which more than anything else will affect its successful outcome."
—William James

Today I was thinking about the various things in my life that are truly rewarding and special. Yes, today the birds were chirping, the air was brisk, and my feet touched the ground with a hop like feel. I thought of how many times in life we question and share the good and the bad.

How many times have you said, "if only", these two words could be positive or negative? I thought of all the people who say "if only" I was "thin enough, rich enough, smart enough etc. Would this really conquer the demons and questions that hold you back. Maybe you thought that you would be able to ... (fill in the blank) once you lost the weight, became rich, increased your learning power, etc. Does this mean that if you do not lose enough weight, exercise enough, wear an outfit at least 2 sizes less than you are, you can't do it or don't deserve it? Do you say, "I will wait to do ... until I..."? There are many facets and underlying themes that reflect this belief, some positive and some negative. I could suggest many possibilities for these thoughts and beliefs, however, today I am calling attention to Attitude.

Attitude has to to with an individual's feeling, opinion or a way of behaving, it describes a mental state. I view Attitude as something of a treasure and believe it to be most valuable regardless of where you came from or where you are in life. How does your attitude affect who you are, what you do, what you say and what you believe you can do?

Attitude is today's Thought for a Lifetime! What seems like a zillion years ago, I ate dinner at Hymans Fish House while on vacation in Charleston, North Carolina. It was noted for its fresh high-quality fish without fancy frills. Upon leaving I picked up their business card and noted on the flip side was printed "Hyman's Motto" which was Charles Swindoll's quote and thoughts about Attitude. In it he called attention to the fact that attitude is more important than fact, life circumstances, etc. It has resonated with me since.

Today I ask you to think about your definition of Attitude. What is it, how do you view it, exercise it, and live it. I believe it to be a positive game changer, do you?
Good Luck!

A LESSON IN ANGER

"Anger doesn't solve anything. It builds nothing, but it can destroy everything."
—Lawrence Douglas Wilder

Today I was reflecting on anger. Something we see and experience in many people and perhaps ourselves, all too often. It is a defense mechanism one in which the outcome doesn't solve anything. In fact, it builds nothing and can destroy everything. It is important to understand it and work to reduce it. All too often anger leads to resentment, another negative reaction causing pain externally and internally. Let us read the following lesson about anger. It is apropos for today's TFL. It is something I saved in one of my multiple files for years.

A Lesson in Anger

There once was a little boy who had a bad temper. His Father gave him a bag of nails and told him that every time he lost his temper, he must hammer a nail into the back of the fence. The first day the boy had driven 40 nails.

Over the next few weeks, as he learned to control his anger, the number of nails hammered daily gradually dwindled down. He discovered it was easier to hold his temper than to drive those nails into the fence.

Finally, the day came when the boy didn't lose his temper at all. He told his father about it and the father suggested that the boy now pull out one nail for each day that he was able to hold his temper.

The days passed and the young boy was finally able to tell his father that all the nails were gone. The father took his son by the hand and led him to the fence. He said, "You have done well, my son, but look at the holes in the fence.

The fence will never be the same. When you say things in anger, they leave a scar just like this one. You can put a knife in a man and draw it out. It won't matter how many times you say I'm sorry, the wound is still there. A verbal wound is as bad as a physical one.

Thoughts for a Lifetime

It is extremely important that we do not repress anger, one that can lead to a toxic state. If repressed it can lead to anxiety, psychosomatic illness, abused feelings, depression and low self-esteem. The major issue is to learn how to control your anger, understand it before you find yourself in a state of pain and confusion. The awareness of this feeling is paramount. James Thurber said, "Let us not look back in anger, nor forward in fear, but around in awareness".

As I write this, issues of anger and malicious intent, are reported in multiple ways. I hope the above TFL will help to call attention to the negativity of anger and the importance of understanding it and making peace with it.

A wise man was asked what Anger is, he said "It is a punishment we give to ourselves, for somebody else's mistake".
—Vybc Source

POWER

"There's nothing good or bad but thinking makes it so."
—Shakespeare

Today's Thoughts for a Lifetime is about Power.

When I read the above quote from Shakespeare it makes me think about how powerful a thought it is. We are driven by multiple events, experiences, and realities. These lead to behaviors and actions both positive and negative. This makes me think of those in power who perpetuate their actions via the need to win a power struggle which can be experienced on both a micro and macro level. What have you internalized, believe in and experienced in your life. What and how does it effect your sense of power.

The dictionary defines power as the ability to do or act in a specific way in multiple areas. It speaks to the power of people, physics, math, science, the bible, politics etc. Today I am reflecting on one's internal and external power, how we see it, and how to use it in positive ways.

This TFL is a statement of choice that I hope will whet the appetite of our thinking and representation of life. The power to believe, forgive, understand and grow is included in my thoughts today. What do you think?

ENJOYMENT

"Enjoyment is not a goal, it is a feeling that accompanies important ongoing activity."

—F. Karl Wilhelm von Humboldt

Today's Thoughts for a Lifetime is about enjoyment. This morning while walking, I experienced a plethora of emotions: sadness, anxiety, happiness, etc. I connected to Pandora selections on my iPhone and immediately a blast of feel-good experience permeated through my soul. A level of enjoyment is what I experience with music; this is a treasure for me. I recognized that I needed further explore the subject of enjoyment.

Questions like:

> What is your definition of enjoyment?
> What do you enjoy?
> Do you allow yourself enjoyment?
> If not, do you know why?

Enjoyment is a feeling, in psychology affect is the underlying experience of emotion, attachment, mood and feeling. Feelings are paramount to acknowledge and understand, especially when you allow them to surface. Perhaps you will agree that feelings wax and wane, they both decrease and increase alternately.

The therapist in me began to question feelings and one's affect. In doing so I was reminded of Dr. Arnold Lazarus' Multimodal Model Approach to therapy. In it he identifies seven modalities (BASIC ID), that make up a relatively simple technique to help deal with one's difficulty to reach decisions. It focuses on reducing suffering and promoting growth.

This is not the venue to explain and explore this in detail, however the affect in BASIC ID deals with emotions, feelings, and moods which are tied to his other modalities. He ascertains that what makes a person experience emotions, feelings and moods are central to one's overall makeup.

My goal today is to offer the above information and to suggest that you become more aware of your sense of joy, and the reality of the importance of enjoyment.

"Pleasure is a shadow, wealth is vanity, and power a pageant; but knowledge is ecstatic in enjoyment, perennial in frame, unlimited in space and indefinite in duration."

—DeWitt Clinton

Allow yourself to enjoy the joys and pleasures of life, do not lose them!

PERSONAL DECLARATION OF INDEPENDENCE

July 4th signifies the anniversary of the signing of the Declaration of Independence in 1777. It became an official national holiday on June 28, 1870, and has been celebrated in multiple ways. Perhaps as you read this, you too are celebrating with family, friends, food, and fireworks.

Today's Thought for a Lifetime is freedom. What does freedom mean to you?

On a macro level, we look around and see too many dichotomies in the thinking and actions of people. We witness extreme differences and individual reasons for them.

On a micro level, we need to look within. Yes, there are many freedoms that might be misdirected or missing. Unfortunately, this adds to anger, frustration, fears, and hopelessness in many. But today I urge you to look at what you are personally grateful for. Let us position ourselves from a positive perspective, not a negative one.

Allow yourself to Stop the pessimism, Look at what it leads to, Listen to your positive inner self and Feel the comfort and peace within from this exercise. Stay with it, recognize it, and allow it to become part of you, which it already is. The outcome of thinking and feeling this way strengthens our freedom and message. It can become a powerful guiding light that can lead to a more positive outlook/outcome.

> "If there is light in the soul,
> there will be beauty in the person.
> If there is beauty in the person,
> there will be harmony in the house.
> If there is harmony in the house,
> there will be order in the nation.
> If there is order in the nation,
> there will be peace in the world".
> —CuriositesByDickens

Let your light shine and reflect on life and love your Declaration of Independence and the world in which you live.

PURPOSE IN LIFE

HAND IN HAND – *"The greatest work has always gone hand in hand with the most fervent moral purpose."*
                    —Sidney Lanier

Today's Thoughts for a Lifetime is a short introduction to the topic of the Purpose in Life, this one is personal. To me purpose includes something I am passionate and enthusiastic about, embracing my sincerity and steadiness of emotional warmth.

I am thrilled to share that my newest book was just published which is a workbook that supplements book one. (Below is more information on this).

I share this because early on my purpose was:

1. To write about loss and grief as it applies to changing one's relationship with food, this can be applied to other obsessional behaviors as well. I believe that this is an untapped area, one that is vital for us to be aware of and understand.
2. The other one was to be a model for my grandchildren, hoping that they would think that if their Nana could write a book, they could pursue anything they wanted to if they visualized and worked at it.

I share how these two purposes led to the completion of not only one book but two. As you read on, I suggest that you to think about your Purpose in Life and pursue it.

"Like the star, that shines afar, without haste and without rest, Let each man wheel with steady sway round the task that rules the day, And do his best."
                    —Goethe

Changing Your Relationship with Food Once and For All: The Ultimate Workbook (2024)

How grief and loss represent the conduit to change and sustain a healthy relationship with food.

23

Thoughts for a Lifetime

This workbook guides the reader through the steps developed in Dr. Parente's book Parting is Such Sweet Sorrow. Saying goodbye to an eating problem. Her 6 step Template for Change addresses issues of grief and loss.

In this workbook questionnaires and responses from past group members will help to clarify the impact of this conflict-ridden relationship with food. Thought provoking exercises and questions you need to think about are presented to get on a path to positive change.

The exercises and treatment modalities will help the reader say goodbye to disordered eating once and for all and begin to enjoy food as it was meant to be enjoyed and valued. Dr. Parente thanks you for all the support and hopes this will help someone in the process.

Link to book: https://rb.gy/a0y3xs.

HOPE

"Hope is being able to see that there is light despite all of the darkness."
—Desmond Tutu

Today's Thoughts for a Lifetime is Hope. As we look around, we find that there are so many things in life that can be viewed as positive and/or negative.

In the book of Ecclesiastes, the focus on the meaning of life prevails. The message and most powerful quote, as I see it, is "There is a time for everything, and a season for every activity under the heavens". It focuses on finding the meaning in Life and the Passing of Time.

The takeaway I am focusing on today is the value of Hope and its importance throughout the Seasons of our Life.

How do you define hope?
What is hope for you?
Do you believe in the value of it?
How do you incorporate Hope into your daily life?
Can you and do you internalize the meaning and importance of it?
Do you hold on to its meaning even in the face of adversity?

Christopher Reeves SPOKE ABOUT NOT GIVING UP, LOSING HOPE OR SELLING OUT, let us never forget that.

In today's Thoughts for a Lifetime, I suggest that you ponder the above. The acceptance of hope and its value is more important than ever. We need to cherish its meaning and see it as a pillar of our human foundation. We need to recognize its enormous value in any life experience we encounter.

"Hope is the pillar that holds up the work. Hope is the dream of a waking man."
—Pliny the Elder

Thanks for listening!

INTENTION/PROCRASTINATION

For several weeks I intended to write a new "Thoughts for a Lifetime", but never did. When thinking about this, I experienced a mixture of feelings as to why I didn't. However, here I am finally putting thoughts to pen, "maybe today I will complete my desire/intention to actually think about it, write it and share it". Here goes!

What is the definition of intention?
What supersedes my intention? Why?
How can I follow through on my intention?

Let's begin with the Merriam-Webster dictionary definition of intention:

"What one intends to do or bring about."
"A determination to act in a certain way: Resolve."
"A concept considered as the product of attention directed to an object of knowledge."

There is a plethora of reasons for our actions in life, in this case, the hesitation to fulfill my intention to write a Thoughts for a Lifetime until now. The scope of intention is varied, simple yet complex, and most likely has its roots in our physical, emotional, psychological, and spiritual life. This differs in each of us.

Today my focus is also on procrastination as it effects intention. What this means, how it affects self talk and the ability to stay focused and in the moment.

Do you Procrastinate? Procrastination is to put off intentionally and habitually. Why?

1. Do you procrastinate due to fear or anxiety?
2. Are you overwhelmed with the task, fear of failure, fear of success, worry about the process, rather than completing the project, not knowing what the future will bring?
3. Do you lack confidence, and do you truly want to complete the

task?

4. Do you believe that you have the control to do so?
5. Poor time management; are you aware of your priorities, goals, and objectives. Are you overwhelmed by the task or are you too busy?
6. Are you experiencing personal or financial difficulties?
7. Are you bored with the project or intention as it is?
8. Are you unrealistic with your expectations, if so this may lead to rebellion in the form of procrastination?

What can you do to reduce or stop procrastination?

1. Recognize if you procrastinate, and you want to overcome it.
2. Ask yourself what you really want and make the decision to make a change.
3. Take action-be mindful of your decision not to procrastinate.

How to do it:

1. Take baby steps, break it down.
2. Imagine how good you will feel once you motivate yourself and follow through.
3. Stay in the Present. Stop, Look, Listen and Feel what is present and respond to what is most important.

It is and was my intention to complete this Thoughts for a Lifetime and to offer you, my audience, some of the insights on Intention and Procrastination that I have experienced and learned from.

Hopefully you will find value in the above in your life personally, professionally, psychologically, emotionally, and spiritually.

I am compelled to end this TFL by repeating a quote I used on Inspiration. I feel it speaks to the above subject. Read it, understand it, digest it and be it.

"Start by doing what's necessary, then do what's possible, and suddenly you are doing the impossible."

—Francis of Assisi

SELF-SABOTAGE

"Our biggest enemy is our own self-doubt. We really can achieve extraordinary things in our lives, but we sabotage our greatness. Because of fear!"
—Robin Sharma (tickledthink.com)

Today's Thoughts for a Lifetime is Self-Sabotage. Do you want to change something one day, yet you keep things as they are no matter how uncomfortable they may be? The reason that causes one to fall victim to this is, in part, self-doubt. Self-doubt can be rooted in fear, shame, anxiety, and inner voices. Inner voices can be internal from within, or external from the outside, from the self and from others.

The theme is wanting change vs. keeping things as they are. I call attention to this in my book Parting Is Such Sweet Sorrow, Saying Goodbye to an Eating Problem. This book deals with some of the causes of codependency and reliance on an eating problem and how it affects loss. Regardless of the effect self-sabotage has on you, it is important to welcome the challenge to not let internal or external criticism rob you of your sense of security.

What do I mean? If you slip or fear that you will, it is a slip DO NOT make it a BLOCK. Make it right, acknowledge the situation whatever it is, and allow yourself to feel positive to continue. This will help your self-acceptance and fuel you. What do you have to lose?

Think positive, do not allow self-sabotage to destroy the essence of your vitality and life. Good Luck!

OPEN EYES

Today I ask you to ponder: Do you go through Life with your eyes open, or do you go through Life with your eyes closed?

Today I was with someone who has Parkinson Disease with Dementia.

This person was extremely confused, and I noticed he was functioning with his eyes closed. When I suggested he open his eyes he did so. The difference was amazing, it was as though a light bulb went on. In my mind when his eyes were closed, he was into his mind/head primarily. Once he opened his eyes he could see outside himself and truly focus; this enabled him to be in the present. This is such a simple act, an act we all take for grant it.

I could explore this and suggest many reasons and possibilities of what this could represent and mean to you, however that is for you to decide. Please ask yourself: Are you and do you go through life with your eyes open or closed?

THE BEAUTY OF LIFE AND THE BUTTERFLY

"Never lose an opportunity of seeing anything beautiful, for beauty is God's handwriting."
—Ralph Waldo Emerson

Today I was inspired to write this thoughts for a Lifetime about the beauty of butterflies and their association with life.

Did you know that rather than flapping their wings up and down like birds, butterflies contract their bodies making a slanted figure eight pattern with their wings. As the butterfly's body contracts, the motion pushes air under their wings, effectively propelling it through the air. The Lifecycle of a butterfly, as you may know, starts in the egg stage-then to the caterpillar stage-then to the pupa stage-then to the adult butterfly. In addition, butterflies have big wings for their body and are much larger than they need to fly. They can fly with half of their wings moving.

Do you believe that we as humans could fly where we want? Has your journey been jeopardized by the belief you were not good enough, smart enough, rich enough, etc.? Are you aware of how your self-love and self-value effects what you do in life? Do you allow others to victimize you, causing self-neglect and avoidance? Has a level of depression and anxiety added to the lack of positive thinking?

Instead: Acknowledge your feelings.
Feelings are temporary, notice when, they are positive.
Recognize that depression and anxiety are a form of expression and not permanent.
Free yourself by focusing on your senses: sight, smell, taste, hearing, touch.
Notice how love and play can affect you, give it a chance.
Notice the importance of facing truths, both positive and negative ones.
Express your desires, hopes and fears.

When you begin to incorporate the above, you begin to live with the authentic part of you; this is freeing and beautiful. Just like the butterfly, you can venture out and return to your safe place. The beauty of life becomes clearer, believe that if you want it, it is truly in your hands.

"Be at one with the beauty of yourself."
—Louise Parente

"Beauty awakens the soul to act".
—Dante Alighieri

COURAGE/FORTITUDE

"It is only through labor and prayerful effort, by grim energy and resolute courage, that we move on to better things."
—Theodore Roosevelt

Today's Thoughts for a Lifetime is about courage also defined as fortitude. What about courage! It takes courage to:

Pursue what you want.
Say No when you want to say Yes because you know it is the right thing to do.
Acknowledge your faults.
Keep quiet when deep down you want to speak out, or
Speak out when deep down you want to hide, deny, or stay silent.
Acknowledge when you are wrong.
Strive in the face of adversity.
Acknowledge that you believe you deserve....

I could continue to write my thoughts and experiences in this area however, the primary theme of this post is to raise the issue of courage/fortitude for you.

Think about how it has played out in your life and how you want it to play out today and tomorrow.

Jeremy Collier states: "Fortitude implies a firmness and strength of mind, that enables us to do and suffer as we ought. It rises upon an opposition, and, like a river, swells higher for having its course stopped."

What does Courage/Fortitude mean to you?

BEING PRESENT

The Vietnamese Buddhist monk and philosopher Thich Nhai Hanh, wrote about the importance of enjoying a good cup of tea. He stated that one must be completely awake, and in the present to enjoy tea. The theme of this message is the importance of being present in life. To focus on today, rather than worrying about the future. The ability to stop ruminating about the past or worrying about the future.

Today's Thought for a Lifetime includes tips and techniques to limit and change thinking errors that rob us of being in the present. They are:

1. All or nothing thinking. Do you view things in black and white categories. If your performance falls short of perfect, do you see yourself as a total failure?
2. Overgeneralization. Do you view and dwell on a negative event as a never-ending pattern?
3. Catastrophizing or minimizing, sometimes called "binocular tricks". Do you exaggerate the importance of things, or negate them?
4. "Should" statements. You are motivated by "should" or "should not" or "must" or "ought to". The consequence of this thinking is emotional guilt. Be aware that if you direct the "should" onto others, you may feel anger, resentment, and frustration.
5. Personalization. Do you see yourself as the cause of negative external events, but you were not primarily responsible for them?

The above thoughts lead to negative feelings and rob you of being in the present. They rob you of life.

Today's tip is to Stop, Look, Listen and Feel and Be Present.
Life is truly a present, treasure it.
I hope you find the above tip of the day to be helpful and thought-provoking.

RELATIONSHIPS

"My best friend is the one who brings out the best in me."
—Henry Ford

"No person is your friend who demands your silence or denies your right to grow."
—Alice Walker

Recently four very special friends came to visit. During that time, we shared memories and experiences of the past. It occurred to me that this visit would also become a memory, one of joy. Yes, this friendship signifies an example of a healthy, long-lasting one.

In past writings, I suggested that the readers become more aware of their relationship with individuals, food, drugs, alcohol, compulsive spending, gambling, etc.

Some relationships can be friendly, positive, or fearful, and painful. There are times we want to change our relationships to a healthy one, yet the attachment is one which renders us helpless.

Perhaps we become comfortable with the discomfort experienced. But is that truly what is needed and desired? If we look deeper, along with a dysfunctional attachment that requires change, comes a fearful and painful separation, one that can lead to freedom. Along with this separation, albeit one you may want and "crave", is the need to understand the feelings and thoughts that accompany it, this is vital. Here again, the subject of loss and its multiple implications surface.

When you decide to make a change, action is the missing link. If you wish to make this change, I ask you to honestly explore the following questions:

"Are you ready and willing to understand and change your dysfunctional relationship?"
"Are you ready to focus on the feelings of loss that will surface"?
"Are you willing to grieve that which surfaces as you go forward"?
Only YOU can decide! But you can!

SENSES

Today I drove to one of my favorite towns in New Jersey. I was playing some of my special music selections from Pandora. As I drove, I could feel the light breeze as it whispered through the car windows. I saw cornfields rich in color and farm stands abundant with fruits and vegetables that I could almost taste causing my stomach to growl with hunger. It occurred to me that the beauty of this drive was enhanced due to the 6 senses I was experiencing: hearing, touch, sight, smell, taste and interoception (hunger).

Life with its ups and downs can be appreciated when we experience some, if not all, of the senses. How easy it can be to forget or avoid some of life's pleasures due to one's circumstances there in. How you navigate life's situations usually affects senses in some way, if you are aware of it. It is both helpful and important to be aware of them and how they are woven into the fabric of your life.

Do you taste what you eat or drink? Or do you eat and drink so quickly you might not remember that you did in the first place. How do you react to what you hear, and smell, what is your awareness and its affect? How does it feel to be touched in a soft, caring way. Any realization could have an up side or a down side, but that awareness opens another though, feeling path. If you focus on this tool in other areas of your life, it can help make that "all important transition" to acknowledgment, health, and peace of a new and healthy relationship within.

This Thoughts for a Lifetime is to remember and focus on your senses in all aspects of life. Our senses are a gift to use and appreciate. Let us not negate, rather appreciate, experience and value as one of the many treasures we have in life.

Thank you!

Abundance · Growth · Joy

THE ESSENCE OF LIFE

Today the my Thoughts for a Lifetime has to do with the essence of your life. Essence is a noun that refers to the quality of something. This quality relates to character, uniqueness, or perhaps the gist of something. It can be necessary, special, crucial or essential.

What is the essence of your Life? I asked this question to friends, colleagues and family, they wanted to be sure of the definition of Essence. Once the definition was clear, the following responses were shared.

The Essence of my Life is:

1. "To be real, I do not have to be something I am not."
2. "To live one day at a time."
3. "To live with consciousness."
4. "To live with intention."
5. "To live with honesty and love."
6. "To live with self-respect."
7. "To go with the flow and discover the wonder."
8. "To find peace in the past, present and future, with self and others, this is love."
9. "To feel the joy of winning a soccer game."
10. "To be independent."
11. "To feel pride in my family."
12. "To feel fulfilled when sharing time with loved ones."
13. For me, it is to believe in Life regardless of what happens."

In today's world, life changes constantly. How you define the essence of your life can help you through the good times and the bad times. It is important to Stop, Look, Listen and Feel to your inner and outer world, something I stress in my writings regarding how to change negative relationships. As we celebrate this holiday season, please ask yourself what is the Essence of Your Life?

This is today's Thoughts for a Lifetime, honor it and be one with it.

Would you like to share what your essence of life is, as well as any thoughts on the subject? Please do so! Thank You!

FRIENDSHIP

"The Language of Friendship is not words, but meanings. It is an intelligence above language."

—Thoreau

Today I was reflecting on friendships throughout my life. I recalled times when I had many acquaintances; that is different than friendships that I have, value and care deeply about. I reflected on those in my life and in the lives of others that I knew or treated in my practice. The virtues of friendship have been defined as someone with Empathy, Loyalty, Trust, Honesty, and Respect. I have always believed that different friends compliment me in different ways, as I would for them. A friend can be sincere, or honest, or intellectual, or giving etc. Each one may be special or perhaps unique in their own way. Some may have many of the virtues stated above, only you know how that affects your relationship with them.

I have written extensively about one's relationship with their abusive behaviors such as with food, alcohol, obsessive and compulsive buying or spending to mention a few. Many of these types of relationships become a problem and how we view them, deal with them, and hopefully work to change them becomes the task. Today I ask you to reflect on your friendships. My intention is to embark on a journey to share my thoughts on how to change a negative addictive relationship via future Thoughts for a Lifetime on this problem.

For today, I wish you friendships that are <u>Friendly, Favorable, Forgiving</u>, filled with understanding and respect and not one that can be described as your <u>Foe</u> (enemy and hostile). Emerson's description of a true friend is someone who can be sincere, someone you can think aloud before.

REACHING THE FINISH LINE

"There are many things in life that will catch your eye. But only a few will catch your heart. Pursue those."
—Anonymous

Today was the New York City Marathon 2023. The energy and desire experienced by the runners is so exciting for me to view. People from all over the world participate and/or experience it. The runners are from different countries, cultures, ages, sexes, and professions, schools etc. The importance of connection, hope, determination, anticipation, and purpose cannot be replaced. The feeling of positivity is sprinkled with optimism which must be preserved and experienced in this life. It is an example that it is never too late to get involved, work toward a goal and replace doubt with hope. Getting to the finish line is the goal but the participants experience something they will retain as they continue their journey through life. This experience permeates to the onlookers as well.

Find your marathon, work at it, get through the difficult times, always keeping in mind that it is never too late to challenge, experience and enhance your sense of self and life.

"It's never too late to do something great."
"Never underestimate your potential. Or discount your ability. Most great achievements are based on perseverance. Believe in yourself. Persist. When others give in, keep going. When you falter, have faith and surge ahead."
—Patrick Lindsey

WORKING/WRITING - RESISTANCE & CHANGE

"Paralyze resistance with persistence."
—Woody Hayes

Today I sat down with the goal to write. My desire to write another book waxes and wanes. I did the same thing two of the previous three days. I eventually break through my resistance, but: Why do I resist, and what is resistance. What do you think about it?

I have written about imagery, procrastination, fear, self-sabotage, etc. Where does resistance fit in? Resistance prevents the creation of the image. It is negative, internally, and externally, it is deceptive, it corrupts and is fueled by self-sabotage and isolation.

Recently I read that procrastination is manifested in resistance, perhaps because we sometimes rationalize it. Resistance is a self-abusive behavior. I see it as an umbrella that is kept open by negativity, self-deception, self-sabotage, procrastination and more; it prevents growth. It may feel like a protection, which it is at times, but it is one that has multiple limitations.

I am quite aware of how I feel about it. It makes me unhappy and negative; it is toxic and can elicit fear. Resistance feeds on fear and the biggest fear is that it will succeed. Primarily resistance has the potential to rob me of a piece of life. It has been described as something we cannot touch or hear, it leads to distraction.

OK, my understanding of resistance is much clearer, but what can I do about it? Some tips follow.

I can acknowledge its existence and its impact on me. For me this step is the main one in the process of making change.

I must clarify what my goal is. Do I and What do I want to write? I need to "brainstorm" what the possibilities are to achieve that.

I need to put things in order, internally and externally. For me, I need my writing materials, notebooks, computer, pens and pencils, reference books and articles and location clearly defined.

I need to fuel my inspiration. For me it is through music which represents the essence of positivity and creativity that harmonizes my prayer and belief system.

I know that I must ask for help when I need it. If I don't, this is a form of resistance.

I have learned that I must be patient, recognize my limitations and learn from criticism.

I need to make peace with my resistance, to follow my life journey and create what I can. I must acknowledge this and give myself credit for it.

The above points will hopefully serve as a reminder of the impact of resistance and the need to believe in your creativity and wisdom. Good Luck!

INNER VOICES

"When to come in out of the rain."

I recently read a short article that referenced "points of common sense", one of which was "Do you know when to come in out of the rain?"

What exactly does this mean? Does it or has it applied to you? Does it make sense to you? My thoughts are many, let's look at some possibilities and how they may reflect your life.

First, to come in from the rain, you need to ask yourself the following:

Are you aware that you are in the rain?
How does it feel to be in the rain?
What does the rain represent?
Are you ready to come in from it?
The rain can be indicative of many things. One of my thoughts (and there are many) is that of control and inner messages. Focus on your inner voices, are they negative, do they keep you stuck?

If you choose to be "rained on", I ask you to ponder the following:

Do you use the power of the word against yourself?
Don Miguel Ruiz (1997), the author of The Four Agreements, calls attention to 4 Agreements that are tools to find yourself and recreate your story the way you want.

His first agreement reads: "be impeccable with your word"; he calls attention "to never use the power against yourself". Do you judge yourself harshly and experience guilt? He states that to be impeccable means that you do not allow the negative voice to abuse you or allow anybody else to go against you. When you feel love and feel good about yourself the emotions of love counter the feelings of envy, anger, and sadness. The outcome is that you do not betray yourself.

His second agreement is to not take anything personally. The awareness that what others may say and do is a projection of their own reality.

42

Stepping back and not reacting to what another says helps not to be a victim of suffering.

His third agreement calls attention to the importance to not make assumptions. Communication with others and the courage to ask and express oneself is vital and can transform your life.

His fourth agreement encourages one to do their best in any situation. This will help one to avoid self-judgment, self-abuse and regret. (Miguel Ruiz, 1997)

For today, think of the above, become aware of your inner positive voice and how it can impact life as it is today and tomorrow. Remember that when you come in from out of the rain you let go of the self-abusive negative voice and replace it with positivity, hope and fulfillment.

Good luck and keep going!

MINDFULNESS & FEELINGS

"Mindfulness is required to be able to see beneath the surface of appearances to what is actually unfolding in your own experience, to what is in your own body, in your own mind."

—Jon Kabat-Zinn

This morning, I got up and began doing what I always do. Today I felt more rushed. Why? Sometimes I understand why, but that wasn't the case today. Perhaps the Why wasn't enough.

I received an iWatch for Christmas, a gift I am beginning to think really picks up messages from me. Up popped the app suggesting a mindful exercise was due. Often, I am too busy to access this however this morning I decided to follow through. My busyness stopped, I sat in my comfortable chair and began to_ experience the restful feeling. Feelings began to pour from my eyes and I allowed them, I remained seated. Once this exercise ended, I began to write this Thoughts for a Lifetime. One of my suggestions to people is to Stop, Look, and Listen in life, something I truly believe can be helpful in many ways. Today I am suggesting an add-on to this; it is to allow yourself to <u>Feel</u>. I did Stop, Looked at what was going on and Listened to myself and then began to <u>Feel</u> within. This exercise allowed me to feel a sense of peace, along with the sense of understanding it. This was an exercise in mindfulness that I needed. It inspired me to write this today.

We read about mindfulness, perhaps understand it and carry it out, but without the realization of how it can be helpful, we could "miss the boat" with how it could be helpful. Ask yourself do you practice mindfulness; do you allow yourself to feel? If you do, what are the results? Of course, they can be different during each day that we live. Yes, I do Stop, Look, and Listen, as well as Feel for and about many things, but today's experience this different. The watch pinged I listened, I exercised my right to be mindful which allowed me to bypass the noise I had been experiencing; I truly reflected and felt that which might have had a negative impact at another time.

Although I could write down definitions of mindfulness, its effect on people, and its history, but my message today is to allow yourself the luxury of it. Today please take the time to: Stop, Look, Listen and Feel.

Thanks for listening. What are your thoughts and experiences on this subject, please share.

YOUR RELATIONSHIP WITH FOOD

When discussing one's relationship with food, I urge people to think about the questions listed below.

1. If these questions resonate with you and you are ready and willing to change your negative relationship, begin by exploring and responding to them. Do you really want to change this relationship?
2. Are you ready to accept the fact that you want to change it and what that means?
3. If not, start a self-dialog to understand the inner conflicts that are at work.

If you do not want to change it or you have self-doubts, ask yourself what you will be losing if you do not and, and what will you be losing if you do?

Each day take as much time that is needed to Stop, Look and Listen and Feel for yourself. Think about what was, what is and what will be.

Your perseverance and intentions will follow. This can go for any problematic relationship in one's life, not just food.

Point of reference: My book Parting Is Such Sweet Sorrow. Saying goodbye to an eating problem addresses the issue of loss and its connection to change. The realization that to change means to let go of the attachment, which was something you relied on, could be the glitch that interferes with your desire to change.

DREAMS

In America, Independence Day, July 4th commemorates the adoption of the Declaration of Independence. It represents freedom, patriotism, bravery as well as family get togethers.

Wendell L. Wilkie wrote: "I believe in America because we have great dreams and because we have the opportunity to make those dreams come true". Today my Thoughts of a Lifetime represents this quote.

Do you embrace your dreams?
Do you believe you can make those dreams come true?
Do you feel a sense of freedom emotionally and psychologically?
Do you allow yourself the freedom to be true to yourself?
Believing is to have faith, acceptance in and capability to do.
Please ponder the above, allow yourself to be free and to believe!

Happy 4th!!

THE GLITCH & CREATIVE EXPRESSION

"Kismet – I do not believe in a fate that falls on men, however they act; but I do believe in a fate that falls on them unless they act."
—GK Chesterton

I sat here tonight in a quandary, why was I spending so much time and energy questioning why I hadn't been able to create a new TFL. I had considered many topics for my next one such as imagination, how to take a stand, looking back, looking forward, the science of feeling calm, etc. Somehow, I did not feel a connection to these or other topics. In a flash the realization that I was experiencing a Glitch in my creative process raced through my mind. A Glitch, I said? Perhaps Glitch was not the proper word but then again it was what I felt within. A Glitch is defined as a malfunction or irregularity of equipment in a system, hopefully one that is temporary. Wasn't my Being a system? Yes, I have been created with cells, a body, a mind all with interconnections, etc. I was experiencing a setback; I needed to understand and explore the word which encompassed multiple feelings especially for me.

I read that Astronaut John Glen, in his 1962 book <u>Into Orbit</u> needed to explain: "Literally, a glitch is a spike or change in voltage in an electrical circuit which takes place when the circuit suddenly has a new load put on it". A new clarity began to surface. Did that apply to me? Yes, there were multiple realities, thoughts and feelings that were surrounding my being, many represented a new load. I began to explore them with a newfound understanding. The realization that I could take advantage of this definition of a Glitch, danced in my mind. PROOF: the creation of this TFL.

In Life we experience much, isn't that part of Life! Once we recognize what we are experiencing, it segways into understanding it and acting accordingly. ACTION is the next step.

Today I ask you to think about this. Have you experienced a Glitch in some form. Acknowledgement of the issue or problem is Step 1 to embark and continue the journey of life. It is this belief and action that leads to a sense of positivity not negativity. I wish you positivity on your journey and to recognize that the Glitches in life are truly Nuggets of growth for you to explore and appreciate.

Thoughts for a Lifetime

"Doing is Dreaming-Do noble things, not dream them all day long: and so make Life, Death, and the vast Forever one grand, sweet song."
—Charles Kingsley

THE EBB AND FLOW OF LIFE

I sat here tonight with a river of thoughts and a river of feelings. I reflected on Thoughts for a Lifetime as The Ebb and Flow of Life. This was reflected in the movement of the river that runs behind my house. A river of water that is sometimes calm and sometimes moving with such energy that the white caps spray a mist of moisture to behold, feel and view. Oh, how mother nature greets us at times we do not expect.

I thought of how this river represents the experiences of life, calm yet rough, high yet low. Our feelings are represented in a similar way and how we see life and the importance of them. I began to recognize how important it is, has been and will be to float with the movement, rather than fight it. The calm after the storm, the freedom after the fight. This represents the ebb and flow of life to recognize, because it represents the steadiness of our very existence.

The ebb and flow of life is represented in a multitude of ways, but today I call attention to the steadiness of the river as an example of the rhythm of life and the strength it represents.

"To keep my health…To do my work…To live!
To see it I grow, and gain, and give.
Never to look behind me for an hour.
To wait in meekness and to walk in power.
But always fronting onward toward the right.
Always and always facing toward the light,
Robbed, starved, defeated, fallen, wide astray.
Oh, with what strength I have, back to the Way!"
—Charlotte Perkins Gilman

A MUSE

Worth

"It is not what the world gives me an honor, praise, or gold. It is what I do give the world, so others do unfold. If by my work through life I can another soul unfold, then I have done what cannot be made good, by praise or gold, one tiny thought in tiny word may give a great one birth, and, if that thought was caused by me, I lived a life of worth."

—Richard F. Wolfe

Today's Thoughts for a Lifetime refers to the subject of a Muse. Many years ago, I had a chance meeting with someone who defined herself as a psychic. Within the few minutes of the introduction, she said "you can still be a muse." No further discussion ensued; she went on her way as I did mine. I must admit that this piqued my interest. In the past I read that in Greek Mythology there were nine sisters, all daughters of Zeus and Mnemosyne, each considered to be a muse and responsible to inspire and guide human creativity mainly in the arts and sciences. Today this can be a person who inspires a creative artist of some type.

But how did this represent me? After additional reading, it was suggested that a muse can be part of oneself, thus a source of inspiration and fulfillment from within; I began to think about how each one of us affects others. I thought how important and special it is to be the source of inspiration from within and to those touched via our interaction. Thoughts of those who inspired and encouraged me on my life journey began to emerge. The muse within depends on our values, beliefs, experiences, and goals, both positive and negative ones.

Today I suggest that you look within, become aware and explore your internal muse. Have you been the source of inspiration? Who has inspired you? I believe that to make a positive difference and inspire others, leads to a life worthwhile. What do you think?

51

FAMILY

"Family is but a part of life.
A Life with love abounds.
And if you question it,
Just look around.
For families come in many ways
All special from the start.
Look, feel and gratify your heart."
—Louise Parente, 2023

Today a feeling of renewal was experienced as I spoke to a family member who I hadn't spoken to in years. The recollection of times gone by, those memories of happiness, sadness, concern, certainty, and realities were renewed. Today's Thoughts for a Lifetime focus on the importance of family, memories, and renewal; these can be families from birth and those created by the special people you allowed into your life. It represents the importance of positivity which, if we are lucky enough, we have experienced. Unfortunately some of these experiences could have been forgotten.

This message represents the importance of stepping back in time. It represents a reminder of personal growth and heartfelt experiences from yesterday, today, and what can be tomorrow. Going forward, think about the message of today's Thoughts for a Lifetime.

THE GREAT RESIGNATION

I recently learned about the Great Resignation (the Big Quit) which is a trend in which employees are leaving their jobs. Economists state it followed the onset of the Covid-19 pandemic which has allowed workers to rethink their long-term goals and careers. In June 2021 approximately 3.9 million Americans quit their jobs. This trend can be seen in Belgium, France, UK, Germany, and China but primarily in America. By some standards, this is a strike on the current and future working conditions. It has produced a global supply chain crisis.

Although there are many points I could explore and state, my purpose today is to look at the major theme of change and its multiple complexities. This touches multiple beliefs which have roots in one's psychological, emotional, and spiritual psyche, with the overlay of the reality of the times in both present and future. In my thinking this opens a plethora of feelings, thoughts, and questions about where one is and where one wants to go and be.

This is yet another testament of Human Behavior. The question I ponder is:

"What do you want to do?"
"Why do you want to do it?" and
"How do you do it?"

These are thought-provoking questions that may aid one in their journey of life. How does one navigate the red lights, green lights, detours, etc. that may be faced?

Today's Thoughts for a Lifetime is certainly not a new one but one that needs to be reckoned with, to make change. The Great Age of Resignation has whetted my appetite to explore this further, perhaps on a macro level. The risks can be many, but a positive outcome can far outweigh them, I would love to hear your thoughts on this! What do you think? Thank you!

TIME

"Gone – Lost wealth may be replaced by industry, lost knowledge by study, lost health by temperance, but lost time is gone forever."
—Smiles 1904

Today's Thoughts for a Lifetime is time. I recently purchased a picture frame that was inscribed with Henry Van Dyke's quote on Time, depicting how time can be "too slow", "too swift", "too long", "too short" but "Eternal" for those "who love". All of which are dependent upon life situations.

No doubt that we are surrounded by multiple messages regarding time. This inspired me to write something about this subject today, perhaps it was time for me to do this.

Some tidbits of information I reflected on included the following:

How many times did I say to myself, "I am wasting too much time".

Perhaps this was true, but I was reminded of all the times I felt that there just wasn't enough time to do all I wanted to do. "Let me accept this!"

Maybe for today I want to spend the time doing nothing (whatever this means to me). Why not? This is not necessarily negative. "Let me accept this!"

Let me not forget that I am always growing and becoming within my time. "Let me accept this!"

How many times did I want to deny or delay feelings of fear, anxiety, or grief. "Let me accept this!"

How many times did angry or frustrating feelings rob me of the time to understand and rectify them. "Let me accept this!"

How many times have I spoken to a friend or family member without worrying about the time? "Let me accept this and never forget it!"

WHY?

Taking time is like a breath of fresh air to nourish and experience a life that seems to pass us by too quickly.

LET US ACCEPT THIS & TAKE TIME

54

DECISIONS & ACTION

Today I will briefly call attention to behaviors that can be categorized as abusive or perhaps addictive at times. I have touched on this fact in other Thoughts for a Lifetime over the years. My book Parting Is Such Sweet Sorrow, Saying Goodbye to an Eating Problem focuses on issues of loss and grief that are part of the process of change. It is my belief that the points I make both in this book and the workbook that followed applies to many abusive behaviors, some of which we want to change. There are many relationships one may have, such as a relationship with food alcohol, gambling, compulsive buying, male or female relationships to name a few.

Today I suggest that you become aware of your decision-making skills to begin the process to facilitate change. Once you decide what that is, the awareness of how it has shaped your life and how you want to change it becomes the first step.

The decision comes first. The action comes next. The acknowledgement of loss and grief follows. Equally & more important is to use your skills and creativity to develop your newfound acceptance and find meaning and joy in it. Please ponder the above and decide to incorporate it into your life.

Think about the fact that this process opens the door to decisions and actions that are worthwhile and healthy.

FUTURE ASPIRATIONS

"One of the greatest discoveries a man makes, one of his great surprises is to find he can do what he was afraid he couldn't do."
—Henry Ford

What are the things you are afraid you cannot do? What are the things you were afraid you couldn't do and could?

Maybe these are thoughts and experiences about the past, present or future. How does this subject resonate with you?

In my mind, the meaning of this quote involves a multitude of life experiences. It is present in the life of every child, teenager, young adult, or older adult. It is an integral part of what we believe in, what we learn and what we want. Within its boundaries one will most likely experience fear, anxiety, anger, and shame on one end. However within its boundaries one will hopefully experience a sense of joy, excitement, acceptance, and peace of mind on the other end.

What does this quote mean to you today? Most likely it is/was experienced in the following:

When a child begins to walk, talk, and begins the separation-individuation phase of life.

When a person begins school and completes the academic year, whether it be elementary school, middle school, high school, college, professional training etc.

When one commits to changing a relationship which is abusive, and addictive.

When one experiences tragedy or loss, and that which follows. The list can be added to depending on the individual.

The ability and resilience to "get through", "accept", "find peace" and continue to pursue what life has to offer is, in my opinion, one of the "greatest discoveries one can make". The pursuance of one's aspiration is today's theme.

A major question to address is the why one does not pursue that which is necessary to attain ones' aspiration. How to move from the thoughts to the decision, to the action, is necessary.

This can be the subject of a future post. The questions are many, all important to explore and act on.

This post is merely to whet the appetite and curiosity of the reader; how would it feel to discover you can succeed at whatever it might be? What is it that inspires you? What is it that keeps you frozen?

Whether or not you wish to continue to post your thoughts on this matter here, please allow yourself to think of the above "Thoughts for a Lifetime". What does this mean to you, how important is it, perhaps questions like these will help you to understand and navigate what follows? "I believe it can". How amazing it would be to discover that you can do what you were afraid you couldn't do.

Thank you for listening!

BUNDLE OF THOUGHTS #1

Embrace Life

Here it is a day after Thanksgiving; the Christmas and Hanukkah holidays are soon to follow, year 2021. Unfortunately, COVID-19 has collided with life as we knew it. It is a time to give thanks and appreciate our life as it is. It has been and is a time when eating and one's relationship with food is constantly in flux. Please embrace the concept that you can be comfortable and enjoy what you eat. Life is too special to lose. Do not let the negative relationship with food or family, or work rob you of life. All the best to all of us!

From Fear to Faith

My message today reflects the following quote by John Paul Jones: "If fear is cultivated it will become stronger, if faith is cultivated it will achieve mastery". Please ask yourself if you wish to cultivate this important and necessary message.

What do you think?

Growth

Over 40 years ago a friend of mine asked "Louise what will you be when you grow up?" This was prompted because I had decided to attend college. That question helped me to realize that I never want to Grow UP rather I want to CONTINUE to GROW. I went on to achieve a BSW, MSW and PHD. I believe there is no limit in life if you embrace that belief.

Think about this and EMBRACE IT!

SELF-SUFFICIENCY

"The life of a man is made up of action and endurance; the life is fruitful in the ratio in which it is laid out in noble action or in patient perseverance."
—Liddon

Here we are into week 2 of January 2024 and the questions, hopes and desires may be many. Perhaps you have experienced losses and challenges that have required you to evaluate the importance of being self-sufficient, this is today's TFL.

Questions such as whether you have been able to take care of yourself, or deal with problems without the help of other people may have come into play.

Below are some facts about being self-sufficient, both pros and cons.

Self Sufficiency is:

Feeling secure and content with self, a deep-rooted sense of stability. It is an affective state in which praise and blame do not affect one too much.

An aspect of well-being. This inner security helps one to feel content with themselves, it leads to psychological health.

It is not to be confused with independence from others. As humans we are social beings, and healthy relationships are crucial for overall well-being.

It does lead to greater resilience and reduction of dependency and a sense of accomplishment and growth.

Praise and blame don't affect self-sufficient people too much, they rarely become too carried away with their own good fortune or self-importance.

Unfortunately, it can lead to isolation and difficulty in forming meaningful connections with others.

Due to a lack or need of support, one may feel overwhelmed at times in need,

Striving for self-sufficiency may lead to expectations that are unrealist.

As I see it, we must strike a balance between self-sufficiency and healthy interdependence with others as well as in life. I strongly believe in the importance of working toward creating balance.

Balance continues to be part of my "Life Journey", is it yours as well?

Best

Like a star,
That shines afar,
Without haste
And without rest,
Let each man wheel with stead sway
Rounds the task that rules the day, And do his best."
—Goethe

HURRICANES OF LIFE

"Upward – Notwithstanding the sight of all our miseries, which press upon us and take us by the throat, we have an instinct which we cannot repress and which lifts us up."
—Pascal 1623-1662

Today's Thought for a Lifetime addresses the Hurricanes of Life. As I sit here and contemplate what my next word is, I am reminded of multiple disasters experienced by mankind within the past few months. There were hurricanes, tornados, landslides, floods, and fires.

For purposes of this TFL I identify them as natural hurricanes of life that disrupt our world. This term is a powerful metaphor for challenges and difficulties we all face at some point in life, whether personal, professional, or social.

Hurricanes are overwhelming forces that test our coping mechanisms and state of being. They test our resilience, faith and courage and can represent strengths and resources within ourselves and others. They can inspire us to create art, literature, music, and writings that focus on our emotions, thoughts, and experiences. We might question these difficulties and ask why, why me, if only, etc. These are questions we may never be able to answer, however your inner strength and determination will lead to accommodation and acceptance of what is and will be.

Have faith in yourself and the journey, don't quit and please see the positivity within this.

"You must live in the present, launch yourself on every wave, find your eternity in each moment."
—Henry David Thoreau (1817-1862)

IN-DECISION

"The risk of a wrong decision is preferable to the terror of indecision."
—*Maimonides*

Today I ask you to think about indecision.

My past two days have been plagued by indecision as to what I want to devote my energy to at this time.

Questions:

Should I pursue this or that?
Do I need to pursue this or that?
What could happen if I make a decision, or do not make a decision about "this or that"? Should I shelve this now and enjoy what life has to offer. Perhaps I could revisit at another time?
Only you, or in this case me, can make that decision.

Please ponder this: David Joseph Schwartz quotes that "Action cures fear, indecision, postponement, on the other hand, fertilizes fear".

Ask yourself if this makes sense? Do you want your indecision to develop into fear? It is as though one negative gives birth to another.

I do not know about you, but just now I have made my decision and will act on it, I hope you will as well.

Thanks.

FROM THE MOUNTAIN

"Climb the mountains and get their good tidings. Nature's peace will flow into you as sunshine Flows into trees."
　　　　　　　　　　　　　　　　　　—John Muir

El Avila is known as "el pulmin de la ciudad" which means the lungs of the city because it serves many functions for residents of Caracas, Venezuela. It is home to the longest cable car ride in the world. It climbs 7,005 feet above sea level and drops down to the other side to the city known as Macuto, a beachfront city. It remained open until the end of the 1970's and reopened in 2018. I recall my trip there in the late 1970's as well as my ride up to the top of the mountain. Visually the beauty was breathtaking, from the parts of the trail the fog formed adding a feeling of moisture, the scents awakened my sense of smell.

While looking out to the right I could see Macuto and the ocean, from the left I viewed the city of Caracas. I saw the cable car I rode up in and would return to and descend the mountain to the City of Caracas.

This was a time of appreciation, a feel-good moment, I absorbed it all while waiting for the time to return to the cable car. I had read that this mountain was thought to contain divine inspiration. The time approached to return and enter the cable car which held approximately six people. As we descended, the sight of the amazing terrain was hypnotic. Like a jolt of lightning the cable car stopped! We were at least 4000 feet in between any form of terra firmer. We stopped taking pictures from the cable car and sat in shock and experienced a feeling of dread. My anxiety heightened; the beads of perspiration formed at the rate of my pulse which merged at one point. How did this happen? From beauty and appreciation came concern, worry and fear. We dangled for at least 8 minutes, but it felt more like an eternity. Once the car started up, the feeling of relief cannot be described. Truthfully, I felt like kissing the ground once we approached our destination.

Then and now, I look back, I survived this beautiful trip of the day which might have ended in a very different way. Once I settled down, I felt grateful for the entire excursion. The reality was that the entire experience was one I will always remember. I didn't think I was taking any chances in my decision to visit this beautiful place. Things happen, many we have no idea of the outcome, yet some we do.

The message of this TFL is that we all experience similar situations, maybe not exactly like the above but you know your experiences. The question I ask you to think about is that life events can lead us to many shores but what I learned was, "it is not the mountain we conquer, but ourselves". Hopefully this is a message of hope we must call upon throughout our life journey. My wish is that this resonates with you and is one you will act on.

RESILIENCE

"Life brings with it an understanding of how you can work toward And achieve a goal, but it isn't until you finally recognize that you Have the answer within you that you can move."
—Parente, 2020

This post has been inspired by the 2021 Olympics. I find myself in awe of the competitors. The level of these athletes' desire to work toward the goal of performing at the Olympics requires so much more than we can imagine. Hearing their stories and experiences have inspired me to talk about resilience. The dictionary defines resilience as "the capacity to recover quickly from difficulties, toughness and the ability of a substance or object to spring back into shape, a type of elasticity and flexibility".

Due to the Covid pandemic and its ongoing concerns, many have found themselves questioning their day-to-day life and future. We can crumble under the weight of these questions, or we can rise to the level of recognizing and believing how fortunate we are to have survived. This is a time to exercise our individual resilience. To allow this I believe we need to take each day and see it as a gift, to be an example to ourselves and those who are part of our lives. The goal of resilience is to thrive and believe in life. So, Let's Live It!

Thanks for listening.

TWO SIDES OF THE SAME COIN

"The Soul is the Voice of the Body's Interests."
—George Santayana

With bright eyes and a good night's sleep behind me, I opened my computer. The first email shared information from members who spoke of events, interests, both new and old. These are members of a mutual professional group that I respect and admire as individuals who are extremely gifted. Here I was on a new journey being valued for who I am and my accomplishments, yet I was experiencing a feeling that I could not understand. Physically my eyes began to tear, my reaction included feelings of doubt about my future abilities. I felt that my soul hurt but I was aware of positive feelings as well; they represented optimism, joy, and wonderment about being in this life space. The pain I felt in my heart represented excitement and anxiety, could I possibly create and contribute as my newfound friends do? After taking a few deep breaths, my parasympathetic nervous system kicked into high gear and my clarity began to surface. My reaction represented two sides of the same coin: excitement and anxiety. This was something I have been talking about for years, here it was for me to acknowledge and experience, it was personal.

During life we experience feelings of anxiety as well as feelings of excitement. In the minutes that followed my email read, I experienced both feelings simultaneously, which took me off guard. I needed the silence to tease out the real meaning of this reaction. Yes, there were both feelings, now I could understand it and work on it.

I know and I want to continue to grow in this new area of my life, thus excitement, yet anxiety caused me to doubt myself. This represented a deeper understanding of purpose for this time of my life. In my mind's eye, the journey was temporarily blocked at first.

The point of this Thoughts for a Lifetime is that in life we probably all have similar experiences. Once it is recognized, and felt, we can direct our energy to what we truly want. If we do not give life a chance, chances are that we will never experience life as we want it. Wishing that the above will represent a helping hand on your journey, I remain as I am today.

MAKING AN EFFORT - THE APPLE TREE

Today's Thoughts for a Lifetime focuses on the importance of making the effort to reach a goal. I hope you enjoy the following, it has touched and taught me so much, hope it will do that for you.

A young man went daily to his fruit tree and lay beneath it with his mouth wide open. The gentle breeze stirred the tree, and the fruit would drop down into the young man's mouth. He loved his fruit tree for the way it dropped the fruit so abundantly to him. One day, he went to the tree and lay down as usual with his mouth open, but nothing happened. The breeze did not blow, so no fruit fell. He lay there for many days, with his mouth open, and still, the winds did not blow the fruit down to him. He began to curse and cry because the tree did not give him fruit.

A wise old man happened by and saw him lying there with his mouth open, crying, having a temper tantrum. "Whatever is the matter with you?" the old man said. "I have been lying here for days, and my fruit tree will not drop her fruit, and I am so hungry", cried the young man. "Well then, why don't you get up and shake the tree? Then you can get all the fruit you need", exclaimed the old man. So, the young man got up and shook the tree, and sure enough, down came the fruit.

And from that day forward, he stopped waiting for fruit to drop down, but instead he shook the tree to get his fruit and never went hungry again.
—Author Unknown

I hope the above resonates with you and helps you to see the need to be involved and work on that which is necessary to accomplish what you want to achieve. Read it, digest it and include it in your toolbox of tools to accomplish the finished project. The reality is we must realize that we must focus and work to accomplish the result of what we want and desire. Believe it and do it!

NEVER GIVE UP!

WINDOWS OF THE WORLD

"The energy of the mind is the essence of life."
—Aristotle

A young couple moved into a new neighborhood. While they ate breakfast, the women noticed that her neighbor was hanging out wash. She noted that the laundry did not seem clean. This happened several days in a row; she questioned if her neighbor knew how to clean her laundry. One morning her neighbor repeated this, however this time the wash looked so clean, she questioned it. Her husband said, "I woke up early and cleaned our windows".

How and what we see holds many meanings and opportunities. How pure and clear is the window from which you look?

Today's Thoughts for a Lifetime is The Windows of the World.

What are your windows to the world? Are you aware of them? How clear are they? There are many windows depending on what our interests are. I think of the different cultures, language, histories, arts, and others.

To be able to view them, visit them, study, and experience them adds to our life. The ability and determination to view and explore contribute to what I call the smorgasbord of life.

To focus and grow, find joy, understand, love, and find purpose is a gift of life. This ability to view and experience accurately is enhanced by one's perception, awareness, and clarity of thought and mind. We all have this ability. Do you see yours?

"I was in darkness, but I took three steps. The first step was a good thought, the second, a good word, and the third, a good deed."
—Fredrich Nietzsche

Autumn

Transition • Change • Maturity

CONTROL

One day last week all was relatively calm, and then the wind began to intensify, the air felt damp, and the alert sounded that several tornados were in the vicinity, thus "take cover". The rain began to fall at a rate unbelievable to me, it looked like Niagara Falls from every window.

Mother Nature was in charge, trees fell, houses were flooded, and cars began to float on roads that now looked like rivers, and lives were lost. We were feeling the effect of a Hurricane, now downgraded to a tropical storm.

Fear and concern were experienced by most. As the hours passed and sunset was followed by sunrise, Mother Nature toyed with our feelings for sure. But now we felt the calm after the storm. She was in control. Yes, today the Thoughts for a Lifetime is control.

Control is defined as the power to direct or run things, some characteristics include decision making, action, planning etc. Let's explore the effect of control in your life.

What does control mean to you?
How do you feel if something or someone is in control?
What does control lead to?
What does the lack of control lead to?
Please think of the experiences you have had.
Today's post is designed to encourage you to think about this subject.

For me control represents a multitude of thoughts and experiences, some of them are positive and propel me to a place of motivation yet others the opposite. Today I want to think about control in my life and how I want to explore this topic. I find that by printing this fact, as I just have, a pathway is opened to begin this process. It is the first step in my decision to …

How about you?

BUNDLE OF THOUGHTS #2

Self-sufficiency and Connection

"No man is an Island"

—John Donne, 1624

Today's thought for a lifetime is self-sufficiency and connection and the balance between them. One question I ask you to ponder is if there is a balance between the two in your life?

Stop, Look, Listen and Feel

It is advantageous to remember that defensiveness shows a lack of confidence. Thus it is important to react by understanding where people are coming from, getting as much information as you can out of interactions and by using my preferred method of Stop, Look, Listen and Feel before....

Children & Food

No matter what age your son or daughter is, the issue of weight can become a problem. Chances are they already have some concerns or questions about weight. Unfortunately some children as young as 5-6 and on may have this on their mind, it is hard to know or believe.

My book Parting Is Such Sweet Sorrow, Saying Goodbye to an Eating Problem. How to change your relationship with food, is not specifically for parents/caretakers but the information presented can definitely be an aid to parents. It may enlighten you to think about eating, pressures and relationships in your life as well, all of which can impact theirs. If this sounds like a possibility why not read and review it. Thanks for listening!

THE FORTUNE COOKIE EFFECT

Last week as I opened a fortune cookie, I became interested in this sweet treat with a fortune one gets when ordering Chinese food. As I opened a fortune cookie, I began to question its history. It did not originate in China but rather had its roots in 19th century Japan. Its concept was brought to the United States, and its meaning is to bring a smile and reflection to the one opening it. These tiny pieces of fortune might represent and add a touch of mystery and humor to the one opening it.

Life brings with it many mysteries, humorous and otherwise, which are depicted in the fortune cookie. Two people could read the same fortune and interpret it differently. Fortune can represent wealth, luck and destiny, all with broad interpretations. It encompasses multiple meanings from events and circumstances to shape one's life.

If you talk about someone's fortunes or the fortune of something, you are talking about the extent to which they are doing well or being successful. Destiny, life and experiences are part of this.

What is your experience and belief of fortune?

SUCCESS

There have been multiple quotes written about success. They involve the definition of Success being the intersection between hard work and luck. In fact, the quote "I am a great believer in luck, and I find the harder I work, the more I have of it," has been attributed to Thomas Jefferson. Although luck and hard work may be major power points for success, many suggest the importance of how people begin life as a pivotal point: where they were born, were they born into wealth or poverty, were they born healthy or with health issues?

There is no doubt in my mind that this subject can be viewed in multiple ways such as:

What is your view of success? How do you measure success?
What is your view of hard work? How do you measure hard work?
What do you ultimately want in your life?

The question of how you get success is another point of interest. Ayn Rand says: "The ladder of success is best climbed by stepping on the rungs of opportunity."

Oliver Goldsmith says: "Success consists of getting up just one more time than you fall."

Another thought I have is that success and hard work is in the eyes of the beholder. Maya Angelou has written that when you care for somebody else that you love, the result will be that you have reached success in your life.

Today ask yourself: What is your definition of success? How important is it? How do you measure it- YOU not the others but YOU?

Oh! One more question: Do you Believe in yourself?

THANKSGIVING

"Some memories are unforgettable, remaining ever vivid & heartwarming."
—Joseph B. Wirthlin

Today I had many thoughts about themes I could write about, however, because Thanksgiving (2022) is only 7 days away, my decision was made. To me, Thanksgiving opens the door to the holidays that follow. It is an annual holiday celebrated in the US and Canada and represents the Harvest and other Blessings of the past year.

We can focus on the many negative or questionable life events, some of which we can understand and some we cannot. However, we can choose to appreciate and experience the people and events that touch our hearts. Life is too precious to waste. Let us take in the abundance of what we have, feel satisfied, and be at peace within as well as with those we are thankful to have in our lives today.

We have only one life to live, live it to the fullest with grace, optimism, and appreciation. W. Clement Stone states "If you are thankful, what do you Do? You share". Please think about this and share this with the universe. Thank you.

MY DAILY MESSAGE

Today, as I prepare to move North for several months, I find myself reflecting on a multitude of things:

How quickly the past six months passed.
How quickly each week passed.
How quickly each day passed.

I find myself thinking about each day and how they seem to slip through my fingers. The phrase "take it one day at a time", resonated with me, especially when I wanted to do more than I did on some of them. I began to question and see how hard on myself I probably was, especially when I would say "I haven't done what I wanted to do" or some variation on that theme. However, there were those days that I felt "accomplished".

What is this all about I pondered? I should know better, right? After all I am old enough, right? Life experiences have shown me this, right? But here I was thinking about yesterday, however at other times I was thinking about tomorrow. Here I go again with the "what if's"?

A "mind light", as I describe it, began to brighten and I recalled the extremely meaningful quote from Ralph Waldo Emerson, let's read it together.

"He said, "write it on your heart that every day is
the best day in the year. He is rich who owns the day,
and no one owns the day who allows it to be invaded
with fret and anxiety. Finish every day and be done with it.
You have done what you could. Some blunders and absurdities,
no doubt crept in. Forget them as soon as you can,
tomorrow is a new day; begin it well and serenely,
with too high a spirit to be cumbered with your old nonsense.
This new day is too dear. With its hopes and invitations,
to waste a moment on the yesterdays".

Wow! I thought, had I forgotten this? This quote touched my heart and sent a feeling of optimism and serenity through my mind and body.

Thoughts for a Lifetime

In life, as we know it today, there are struggles, disappointments, and fears, however, there are joys, optimism, resilience, and hope as well. In my thinking it is far better to take each day and look at it as a gift. When I receive a gift, I want to handle it with care, look at it with appreciation and use it in my best interest.

My main message today is to be mindful of what we have each day of our lives. Let us appreciate not depreciate each day we have. What do you think?

INTERNAL BOSS OR LEADER

"Have you heard that people do not leave companies. They leave bad bosses?"

Today's Thoughts for a Lifetime addresses the subject of our internal boss and internal leader. The media and interpersonal connections address the differences between a boss and a leader, many of which have been extremely beneficial. Today my focus is on our internal boss and leader. Do you know the difference? Read each point below to see if they resonate with you. Are you aware of them, and are you aware of the impact they have?

The Internal Boss focuses on fear/anxiety.
The Internal Leader focuses on and inspires confidence.
The Internal Boss focuses on blame.
The Internal Leader acknowledges the situation.
The Internal Boss focuses on and is controlling and rigid.
The Internal Leader is empowering and realistic.
The Internal Boss is guarded and withholding.
The Internal Leader is secure, honest, and open
The Internal Leader is trusting, and naturally loyal to the self.

The goal of this Thoughts for a Lifetime is to:

Make you aware of the above.
Help you to understand your internal thoughts and actions.
Question which of these internal messages are positive or negative.
Ask yourself if you want to make a change, if so, what do you think the outcome will be.
Understand how your internal critic takes away from the self.
Do you suffer from the imposter complex.
I urge you to read this internal Boss and Leader. This awareness leads to change, do you want it? Nourish the Leader in you!

MY SPIRITUAL GIFT

Tonight, as I sit in the loft of my home and listen to The Long Journey by Andrea Bocelli, I am moved by the sounds and the meanings portrayed in this beautiful movie. The message and meaning elicit my feelings of passion for music and life. Music influences the senses as well as the messages of hope, faith and life that tug at my heart. Perhaps a piece of this is because I am of Italian Heritage and feel a connection to what I am viewing. Oh how fortunate I feel to experience this.

Today's Thought for a Lifetime is to call attention to the many gifts we have if we look around us. I see so much beauty amidst sadness. For me, it is important to remember, know and feel this. My husband rests in his bed with limited time to live. I am sure, more now than ever, that my desire to write these TFLS over the many years of his illness was and is a gift that I was given. I cannot define it any other way, I believe it was mine to have and share.

This is a Spiritual Gift that I have received, continue to have, and will feel throughout this journey of my life.

GOOD BEGETS GOOD

There is no doubt that life presents a plethora of events and situations, some are positive, yet some negative. All we need to do is turn on the TV, computer, read an article or engage in a conversation and hear news that elicits negativity and/or positivity. Below is one that represents positivity. When I experience a "feel good" story I want to hold on to it and spread it to the universe.

A relative and his wife were off to the airport, where they were going to Disney World to meet their family. I'll call them Joe and Jane. Jane began to feel ill when she arrived at the airport. She was holding on to the hope that this would not cause a delay in the trip. Simultaneously, a frantic plea to purchase two tickets for a family of eight was heard but unheeded. In fact, the individual was pleading, he offered to pay $500 for the tickets but it was ignored. Simultaneously, Joe, who now saw that Jane was not able to leave on the same flight, decided to change their departure date. He offered their tickets to this family, who now felt relieved and joyous. Joe changed the date of their flight and was happy to do so. He was offered the $500 but he and Jane were happy to help them at no cost.

End of Story? NO

Joe, who willingly did a good deed, was not expecting anything in return. Guess what! The airline personnel overseeing this series of events offered Joe and Jane each a $1000 voucher for future flights. This, they graciously accepted. The theme of "good begets good" has left me with appreciation for the kindness of strangers.

Please pass this story on, we need to hear it. By the way Joe and Jane did get to Disney and are enjoying their family as I write this. Thanks for listening.

BALANCE & CURIOSITY

"The important thing is not to stop questioning, curiosity has its own reason for existing."

—Albert Einstein (1905)

Interestingly I was curious about the subject of curiosity which surfaced several times lately. I have always noted that individuals of any age appeared to have (what I call) a curiosity quotient.

What is curiosity I queried? I understand it as an innate desire to know, explore and understand. It certainly contributes to ones learning and discovering. It can be manifested in many ways, curiosity about people, cultures, intellect, or anything around us. Have you noticed how many young children display their curiosity about the world around them, how they connect socially and emotionally. These traits grow as we grow. To be curious could open a door to a rewarding journey.

Practicing curiosity can enhance the spirit of one's life. My belief is that we are always growing, thus being curious cultivates the drive to learn. Do you:

Ask the why, how, what if questions?
Challenge yourself to understand?
Explore?
Remain open-minded?
Engage?
Play?
Practice mindfulness?
And much more.

Counter to the positive aspect of curiosity can be:

Risky
Overwhelming
Frustrating
Intrusive
Distracting

Louise Parente

Curiosity and most life experiences are not all good or all bad. Balance and the ability to stay focused enhances one's life lessons and the reduction of thinking errors such as catastrophizing, jumping to conclusions, should statements, labeling and mislabeling and others. Curiosity mixed with balanced thinking adds to positivity, something we need more of today and tomorrow.

The above points on curiosity and balance is the tip of the iceberg in understanding, exploring, developing and the impact it has on our lives. Ponder this, how do you define it, how do you balance it, and how do you want to understand and live with it in your life?

"Be curious, not judgmental".

—Walt Whitman (19th century)

NEW BEGINNINGS

"With the new day comes new strengths and new thoughts."
—Eleanor Roosevelt

This week I took my neighbor, who is moving. We went our town's lovely Tea House and Restaurant. As I entered, I felt as though I was transported into another time and place. I was surrounded by its lovely Victorian decor. The delicacy and detail of the surroundings were bursting with color, the feeling of serenity was wonderful. In the entrance was a huge upside-down decorated Christmas tree with beautiful pieces. Each of the ornaments were messages of the past yet here I was in the present admiring them. This felt like a gift, as my neighbor was throughout the years that I have known her.

As we chatted, sipped tea, and ate a lovely lunch, the subject of moving on was shared. Life as it was, is and hope to be, was shared. We discussed how the journey of life can take us down many roads.

Hopefully we all can use our past and present experiences to move to a new positive place. For me messages of hope, faith, joy, pessimism, optimism, action and others were whirling around my mind. We could have explored the many issues of life change but today the joy and experience about her move was the reason for our get together.

The message I want to leave you with today is that "life changes and how we understand and experience each represents a new beginning". How you lived, live, and want to live is the question. Because each phase has a beginning. What is your Expectation & Attitude?

WRITTEN WORDS TO REMEMBER

The following are words that I have heard many times, they go something like "all good things come in small packages". As I ponder this idea, I have a plethora of thoughts. For me, the following thought that pops up, is how many times have I quickly written down a thought for a possible book, lecture, or article. Many times, the thought is written on a small scrap of paper, or a notebook that I can retrieve immediately. For me, I know that if I don't write the thought immediately, I may forget it, life just seems to get in the way. If I remember it later and then write it down, there is a very good chance that the emotional, intellectual, or spiritual meaning will lose some of my intentional drive to write it in the first place.

Ok, so now I have these thoughts in various places but how do I proceed from this point; how do I organize myself? Something that helps me is to take each thought and write it out on a separate large index card.

These cards are large and clear and easier to put in some order. This order helps my intellectual brain to access my feeling brain. In a sense this action helps me to integrate the thoughts and feelings to produce, in words, my original intention. Unfortunately, if I do not proceed as stated, I may lose the thought completely. I could write about the multiple reasons why "I do or do not" do the very thing I wanted in the first place. But today's message is to help one to become <u>AWARE</u> of your action when it relates to writing.

To summarize: those scraps of paper, for me, represent the thought that "all good things come in small packages". However, if I do not organize these thoughts in the hope of producing a larger, more concise message, they get lost in time. Have you experienced this predicament? Hopefully the above will whet your appetite for further analysis and positive solutions. Good Luck!

EAT WITH COMFORT

Perhaps you have been plagued with issues of weight and size for days, months or years. The question is that of being comfortable with yourself. Do you obsess, focus on this issue or similar ones? Do you realize how this thinking reduces your lease on life?

Here it is a day after Thanksgiving, the Christmas and Hanukkah holidays are soon to follow. Unfortunately, COVID-19 has collided with life as we knew it. It is a time to give thanks and appreciate our life as it is. It has been and is a time when eating and one's relationship with food is constantly in flux. Please embrace the concept that you can be comfortable and enjoy what you eat. Life is too special to lose. Do not let the negative relationship with food rob you of life especially at a time that Covid has caused so much loss.

Let us journey through this course of time with ts illness, loss and concern, allow yourself to participate and value life, it is a gift, hold it close to your heart.

DEFINING FEELINGS

"I hear and I forget. I see and I remember. I do and I understand."
—Confucius

Today's Thoughts for a Lifetime includes a few tips on the role of feelings. What is a feeling?

A feeling is a response that occurs on a non-intellectual level.Feelings are subjective and cannot be verified by someone else.

Feelings spur us into action often for self-preservation, an example is when we touch something hot-we draw back our hand to not get burned.

If something makes you feel unhappy- we act by changing the situation or pulling away, whatever it takes to save our psychic skin.

Remember that unpleasant feelings can serve a healthy purpose as well. They allow one to act and attack the problem. One example of this is to attack anxiety by confronting it.

Moods: learn how to understand and avoid things that trigger negative moods and learn how to tolerate your mood.

Fears: can block out other emotional signals, these can be positive or negative, examples are joy, anger, sorrow, fear of failure and/or fear of success.

Depression: if you feel depressed, use alternate healthy methods to help.

An example of this is the 3 N's :

Say NO to unreasonable demands.
Do something NEW.
Do something to NURTURE yourself.

Hope you find the above Tips of the Day helpful and thought provoking, they are only the Tip of the Iceberg.

THE POWER OF WORDS & ACTION

"THE IDEAL LIFE is in our blood and never will be still. Sad will be the day for any man when he becomes contented with the thoughts he is thinking and the deeds he is doing, when there is not forever beating the doors of this soul some great desire to do something larger, which he knows that he was meant and made to do."
—Phillips Brooks (1835-1893)

Today's Thoughts for a Lifetime is the power of words and action. What we say and how we say it can make the difference in our ultimate goals. The phrase "words are cheap" signifies a powerful meaning to me. It represents the fact that one can say something freely but never work to attain it. Example: Do you say, "I want to learn a language" instead you need to say, "I want to complete a beginner course in the language by the end of this year". This requires writing down a goal which is specific and thus more achievable.

Below are some basic steps to help you attain your goals:

> Write down action steps to achieve your goal.
> Schedule and commit to them.
> List possible obstacles or challenges that might arise during this process. Devise a plan to deal with and overcome these obstacles.
> Have self-compassion. There is no need to experience self-anger and frustration which could lead to the termination of the project. Learn from them, adapt to this, and continue to work toward the goal. Too often in life we give up before the completion of the goal, that might have been attained if you followed through a bit longer.

Once you remain on the course and attain your goal, allow yourself to acknowledge it. Do not negate what you have attained. Not only have you achieved your goal, but you have enhanced your sense of self and positivity. You have established a roadmap to achieve future success.

Thoughts for a Lifetime

"Star Gazers – Ideals are like stars, you will not succeed in touching them with your hands, but like the seafaring man on the desert of waters, you choose them as your guides, and, following them, you reach your destiny."
—Carl Schurz(1829-1906)

IMAGINATION

"The world of reality has its limits; the world of imagination is boundless."
—Jean-Jaques Rousseau

Today's TFL is about imagination. Recently I came across the name of a park called Imagination Kingdom in New Jersey. A place with swings, multiple obstacle courses, baseball fields etc. This sounds like a wonderful venue for children of many ages. For me today, it represented a place where children could use their imagination, explore, release energy and other such expressions. I reflected on how important it is to explore our imagination at any age. Memories of exploring Disney World in Orlando Florida began to surface. I recall how I described it as a place of fun, release, exploration for any age. It represents an escape from the many more difficult realities that are whirling around. Today we are surrounded with so many things both positive and negative. How we see and approach aspects of our life can reflect the path forward. I believe we need to instill the belief in positivity amid negativity. Imagination is a built-in trait that helps to accomplish this.

The dictionary defines imagination as a means of forming new ideas or images of external objects, not always present to the senses. Our minds can be creative and resourceful, it is the combination of sensations, feelings and thoughts that can inform. They can be imagined or recreated from past experiences as well as future changes. Imagination is reflected in creative writing, art, acting, and playing music. It is the "stuff" that allows change and development.

Today my message is to nurture your imagination for it is the gift that keeps developing and giving. History has given us people like Leonardo da Vinci, Thomas Edison, Archimedes, Benjamin Franklin, Hedy LaMarr and others. They had the ideas and determination to follow through with their thoughts and to think outside the box and to imagine it. Allow yourself to unleash your creative imagination in whatever area of life you desire. The ability to do so can lead to more optimism in general, something we all need more today and tomorrow.

Remember everyone has an imagination, this is a power of the human mind. Let's explore it, value it, feel it and appreciate it.

Louise Parente

"All grand thoughts come from the heart."
—Vauvenargues

HAPPINESS

"HOME GROWN-Happiness grows at our own firesides, And is not to be picked in strangers' gardens."
                                              —Douglas Jerrold

What is happiness?

Where do you find your happiness?

We all deserve happiness; do you believe that?

Do you expect happiness in your life, and do you desire it?

If you do, make it so.

Happiness is an emotion of joy, well-being, satisfaction, and fulfillment that reflects the pleasure of doing what you like and feeling it matters. It is an outcome of connecting. Happiness is being grateful for the shadows and the lights of life. Happiness is a state of being and a state of mind.

Can one find happiness during times of loss and pain. Happiness represents serenity, thus yes, it is there if you access it, feel it and allow it.

As the holiday season begins, my memories of Christmas are many: Santa coming to our home, being with family and friends, enjoying the many tastes on the table, the religious meaning of this holiday and the coming of the New Year a few days later.

As we approach the holidays, a light in the mist of many shadows renders happiness to shine through. May your holidays be filled with Happiness, Joy and Positivity.

QUEEN ELIZABETH II

The sky was clear, the air slightly heavy, the clouds bellowed with a slight breeze that whispered both joy and sorrow. The crowds were amazingly large, they lined the streets for miles, they were calm and respectful. Looking closer, one could see drops of tears from many.

What was this? It was the funeral held for Queen Elizabeth 11, born April 21, 1926, and died September 8, 2022. She was a wife, mother, grandmother, and great grandmother. Her reign as a queen was 70 plus years. It has been written that Queen Elizabeth had a deep sense of religion, and civic duty. She was a patron of 600 organizations and charities. According to the 2021 Gallup poll, she remained the third most admired women in the world. Her personality has been described as "individualistic".

Today I want to give tribute to this woman who clearly made an impact during her life. I could write about her views, interactions, family involvement etc., but rather the description of "Individualistic" resonates with me.

What does it mean to be individualistic in a world that seems to thrive on exposure and the increasing interaction of social media?

How would you describe yourself, and would the term individualistic have meaning for you?

How has the past affected the present and perhaps your future views?

Have you allowed yourself to accept who you are, regardless of the views of others.

How would you describe your personality, what effects it, and how you see it?

I believe that I am still a work in progress, regardless of age. Do you? Perhaps you are a Queen or a King in your own rite, or perhaps not. Regardless of your answer, the value of knowing, understanding and accepting yourself is golden, this is my closing "Thoughts for a Lifetime" today. Thank you for listening.

THE ITCH

"When we are no longer able to change a situation-we are challenged to change ourselves."
—Viktor E. Frankl

What is an itch?

An itch is an uncomfortable sensation on the skin. Usually, we tend to scratch that feeling to eliminate it. Receptors on specialized nerve cells convert that message into an "itch". We know that there is a link between the nervous system and itching. The scratch can reduce the sensation of the itch, or it may not. The literature states that if you do not scratch the itch, it makes the itching worse, I beg to differ. Be aware of the feeling but do not scratch it, rather wait, and focus on it. Usually, the feeling changes from an itch to a needle like pain. Stay with it, you will experience that the pain and itch is no longer noticeable in a relatively short time.

You may be wondering why I am writing about this? For years, in writings, in treatment settings and with people interpersonally, I have suggested "Do not scratch the itch." In these situations, the itch represents emotional or psychological pain. It is my belief and experience that it is better to acknowledge the pain and work through it rather than avoid it through dysfunctional use of food, alcohol, drugs, gambling, overbuying, etc.

Those actions represent a temporary fix, but not one that is positive and permanent.

Allow yourself to feel it, that feeling will pass, you will feel emotionally fulfilled with hope and gratitude. You will start to understand your actions, and not deny them. Is it difficult to proceed this way? Only you can answer that but be assured that with this change the long-lasting results will be positive.

This action, change in thinking and behavior is tied into what I call my STOP, LOOK, LISTEN & FEEL APPROACH TO POSITIVE CHANGE.

SUGGESTION: Why not focus on the above, try it and see how it resonates with you and your future emotional and psychological situations.

Remember: "There is nothing permanent except change."
—Heraclitus

FOOD, LIFE, LOVE AND LOSS

Food, and the relationship we have with it is different for each of us. This relationship can be enjoyable, loving, painful, abusive, restrictive etc. However, if the relationship with food has caused more pain emotionally, physically, and spiritually, the emphasis on change and how to do that becomes the question.

First ask yourself if you want to change the part of your relationship with food that is abusive, unhealthy, and negative. Changing this requires self-resilience and the ability to understand and find meaning in life. The need to normalize and develop hope are aspects of positive change. There is a loss when change occurs, this is normal not a surprise. To grieve the loss means you may feel denial, anger, depression, fear, anxiety, and shame. I urge you to understand that the outcome outweighs the temporary discomfort you might experience. Please take note that when one door closes another one opens.

Be mindful that negative thoughts will surface and know that you can change them, you are in control. Please, remember that negative thoughts might surface but you can change your reaction to these thoughts, you are in control. This will fuel your decision and acceptance for a healthy relationship with food.

Good luck on your life journey and growth.

INSPIRATION

"Start by doing what's necessary; then do what's possible, and suddenly you are doing the impossible."
—Francis of Assisi

Tonight, I returned home from attending a concert performed by the Bee Gees Now group. While enjoying the show, the audience around me were joyful, energetic, and clearly reminiscing from days gone by, in fact some were dancing in the isles. I reflected on the history of the original group and noticed that this music was clearly a form of inspiration for many.

Yes, today's Thought for a Lifetime, is Inspiration, which is defined as a feeling of enthusiasm one gets from something or someone, often leading to new and creative ideas. For me, music has always been a vehicle of inspiration and tonight the audience reaction to this concert has inspired me to write about inspiration. Examples of other inspirations are found in, life, leadership, motivation, speeches, quotes, bible leaders and your experiences.

My thoughts and questions are many:

What inspires you?
What does that inspiration feel like?
Do you pursue it and if you do, how? If you do not, what is your take-away from that?
Often inspiration can begin a thought that leads to an action, and a feeling.
In my mind, to be inspired is healthy and positive. It may represent the solution for something, or the beginning of something new.
Inspiration and the choice to explore it opens the mind, regardless of the outcome. It is far from static, it represents movement. Whatever the outcome is, it means you explored it, tried it, and had faith in your decision to pursue it. It is not an "all or nothing" approach, it is part of the human experience.

Thoughts for a Lifetime

The message of this Thoughts for a Lifetime is that Inspiration requires the willingness to be, allow yourself to explore this amazing gift of life. Good Luck on your journey!

ON BEING HUMAN

Do you lead a meaningful life that you cherish with others? Let's be aware of human values and develop inner peace.

Today I questioned and read what it means to be human. To be human requires the willpower to decide, to have emotions and knowledge. It represents the experience of life in all its "colors and all its potential". As humans we experience happiness and suffering. These are two sides of the same coin.

Some people say suffering helps one to see what normally they do not wish to see. Philosophers such as Aristotle, Plato, Vedanta and a plethora of others have their own definition of being human. This subject can be explored and understood in hundreds of ways. Today's Thoughts for a Lifetime is to understand what being human means to you. How do you define your characteristics, strengths, and weaknesses. How do you conduct yourself during these times? How are you influenced by self-perception and experiences?

Tony Robbins states that it is important to be an excellent example of being human. Dali Lama states, "Love and compassion are necessities, not luxuries. Without them, humanity cannot survive".

Again, the question I ask you today is: What is your understanding and view of being human and where are you in the mix?

BEING GRATEFUL

"Gratitude can transform common days into thanksgivings, turn routine jobs into joy, and change ordinary opportunities into blessings."
—William Arthur Ward

The clouds were gray, and the air felt damp as I started the motor to begin my drive, then came some drops. The rain began to stream from the clouds and hit the windshield, and suddenly drops of tears from my eyes began to stream down my cheeks. Yes, these were tears of sadness, an emotion characterized by loss, or sorrow, but they were also tears of gratitude, a quality of being thankful for having experienced that which was.

What is gratitude, what does it mean and how is it manifested? These are questions I pose to you today. Today's Thoughts for a Lifetime is just that. In life we experience a plethora of things, some can bring us negativity and sadness, while others can bring us optimism and spiritual awakening. I believe it is imperative that we view these life experiences for what they are, to deepen our gratitude for them and the effect they have had on our lives.

A technique I use when something unexpected or perhaps expected occurs, is:

STOP – take a step back, do not think and act impulsively, wait and then,

LOOK – at what is happening in this moment with yourself and that which surrounds you, then,

LISTEN – to yourself, be present and allow yourself to,

FEEL – what you experience at this time.

It is through these steps that you may experience multiple feelings such as sadness, happiness, optimism, negativity or any other feeling. Permit yourself to be grateful for the experience and the reality of life.

Remember: That gratitude helps us understand our past and is responsible for peace today, as well as the creation of a vision for our future tomorrows. (Melody Beattie)

97

#2021 REFLECTIONS

As the year 2021 comes to an end, I find myself reflecting on a plethora of experiences and thoughts therein related to this time. Due to the impact of Covid and other experiences, the topic of Life and its meanings to me ring loud and true – they are very powerful.

I have learned that:

> Life continues to be important to me and I will not give up on it.
> I know that I have a lot of living to do especially in the face of those I have lost and am losing.
> Life can pass me by in a blink if I don't stop, reflect on it, and live it.
> We all want different things in life. I can only help those who want help.
> If I open my heart and mind, I can see, hear, taste, smell and touch life and it will touch me.
> Due to persistence and patience my book Parting Is Such Sweet Sorrow. Saying goodbye to an eating problem. How to change your relationship with food was published, yeh!
> If I have faith to withstand the perils of what surrounds my life and my work, I can truly continue to live it.
> Life is a journey and I have been so fortunate and grateful for it and what it represents.
> Amazingly some of the painful and negative experiences in Life lead to some of our greatest strengths.

Please remember that:

> After the rain comes the sun.
> After the darkness comes the light.
> After the winter comes spring and summer.
> After crying comes laughter.
> After hopelessness comes hope.
> After restlessness comes serenity.

Victor Hugo stated: "Life is the flower for which love is the honey".

Louise Parente

Let's hold up our glasses filled with the nectar of life and welcome the year 2022. Happy Holidays!
WHAT ARE YOUR REFLECTIONS OF 2021, YOUR THOUGHTS ARE IMPORTANT, ACKNOWLEDGE THEM.

Winter

Rest • Peace • Reflection

THE KINDNESS OF FRIENDSHIP

"INDESPENSABLE – So long as we love, we serve. So long as we are loved by others, I would almost say we are Indispensable, and no man is useless while he has a friend."
—K.L. Stevenson

Today's TFL is titled, The Kindness of Friendship. A few days ago, I decided to see the 1946 movie, "It's a Wonderful Life" with Jimmy Stewart and Donna Reed. This was a movie I viewed multiple times in my life, it always touched me emotionally. The theme reflected the value and the beauty of friendship in its many forms. My thoughts reflected how beautiful and rich it is to have a friendship, old and new.

A friend is:

> Someone who is honest and sincere.
> Someone who will help to pick you up when you fall.
> Someone who you may not see often but it feels as though you saw them yesterday.
> Someone who knows you will be there to support and care about.
> Someone who shares meanings, not just words.
> Someone who has been a gift in your life, just as you have been in their life.

As I write this during Christmas week, I reflect upon many close friends who are no longer here. The value of these friendships include my memories of the past, present and what will be in the future.

Today my message is to value and embrace your shared friendship(s).

A message from It's a Wonderful Life, states that no man is a failure who has friends.

My addition to this is no man is a failure who is a friend. Enjoy and Cherish!

TOUCHED BY LIFE

"Dost, thou love life? Then do not squander time, for that is the stuff that life is made of."
                                                                —Franklin

Touched by Life is a sentiment I find myself thinking about today. It reflects Life's gentle touch both tender and fierce, joyful, and sorrowful. It is different for each person, it is the exemplification of each breath we take, of the grace and dance of life we experience.

As I look back on the year 2024, I am reminded of times both positive and negative, the beauty of simple moments and the strength in adversity. The acceptance of life's moments gives way to emotions and experiences reflected in my rich and versatile source of inspiration.

As we welcome 2025, let us be reminded about the above and let its meaning permeate the Tapestry of Your Life. Happy New Year- 2025.

TODAY I LOST A BEST FRIEND

"In the end, it's not the years in your life that count. It's the life in your years."
—Abraham Lincoln

The lights were low during my conversation with my friend's daughter. My heart ached as she described her mother's lack of consciousness. She and I could not understand how someone who always took good care of herself, someone who would set up her physical examinations months earlier and someone who loved life, family and friends could be on her death bed. Within seconds, a cold feeling crept over me, my heart skipped a beat and, yes, she passed during this time.

I recalled that a few months earlier she discussed how she felt about her life, a life she said she "wouldn't have wanted any other way." How special this discussion was for both of us. I found abundant peace in this.

Today's Thoughts for a Lifetime is about Life, one we pray will be full. Life has its Ups and Downs. There are some things we can plan but many we do not or cannot plan. I believe we all experience a plethora of things, good, bad, negative, positive and others in between.

My thought today also focuses on the importance of acknowledgment, belief and acceptance. To me, these are gifts in life, they are meant to pad our life journey. Think about this, dissect it and allow the thoughts and feelings to permeate. Nothing is really one way or the other. We must strive to develop balance in it any way we can. Just like my friend, she accepted her life events, many that were far from perfect but others that were. She had made peace with her impending passing. Again, how you view your life makes a major difference in how you live life.

Maya Angelou spoke on this subject in many of her writings. One poem stated that no matter how bad life seems today, there is always a tomorrow. Oh, how I wish my friend had a tomorrow to live and share.

This Thoughts For a Lifetime is Dedicated to E, how special it has been to share her life.

TAPESTRY OF LIFE

"We live in deeds, not years, in thoughts, not breaths. In feelings, not in figures on a deal. We should count time by heartthrobs. He most lives who thinks most, feels the noblest, acts the best."

—Philip James Bailey

The Tapestry of Life is a metaphor that describes the interconnected nature of our relationships, experiences and circumstances that shape our life. It suggests that life is like a woven fabric made up of threads that represent different aspects of our lives. These ultimately create patterns that are unique to each of us. In many ways it also speaks to the connections and influences we have with one another.

My mind shifted to our human values such as health and wellbeing, knowledge and understanding, peace and harmony. From this I began to focus on two powerful emotional states, namely inspiration and desperation. "Why these I queried?" Yes, each did represent an aspect of our lives that influences actions and outlooks, but what did it mean to me now? Ahah! Here I was in the final stage of completing my second book, a workbook, which seemed to be taking "forever to me." Emotionally I felt both desperation and inspiration. The beads of perspiration that trickled down my forehead represented stress, urgency and anxiety, all desperation. This was coupled with excitement, joy, and a sense of purpose, and heartfelt, all inspiration. Wow, I thought, these exemplify both inspiration and desperation, each represented a different state, yet they both serve as a motivation to achieve an important goal.

My TFL and theme is to become aware of experiences and how they shape the Tapestry of Life. What do you think? What is your experience?

"There is nothing good or bad but thinking makes it so."

—Shakespeare

CHALLENGES & OPPORTUNITIES

In life we are faced with many challenges as well as opportunities. Life can be beautiful but also be filled with pressures and insecurities.

Today's TFL addresses life challenges and opportunities.

As we approach the year 2024, I find myself reflecting on the above, namely the connection between challenges and opportunities that we face in life. Below are some of my random thoughts, what are yours?

It has been said that a wise man will make more opportunities than he will find. How do these opportunities reflect your life? Sometimes we view things in a larger form, believing they are greater than they are. Sometimes we view our troubles in a smaller form, thus enabling us to focus on the larger reality.

Do you concern yourself to do ordinary things or do you do ordinary things in an extraordinary way?

Do you make use of the qualities and the opportunities that may be a result of them?

Do you persevere and tackle the challenges and troubles that come your way?

Do you believe in the power of your strength and will?

Oliver Wendel Homes stated that in the process of life we sometimes sail with the wind and sometimes against it, "but we must sail, and not drift nor lie at anchor".

How you view life has a profound effect on your life's journey.

"Dost thou love life? Then do not squander time, for that is the stuff that life is made of."
—Franklin

Let us focus on the beauty of life and its many wonders as you begin the Year 2024. Happy New Year!

IMAGERY

The ability to visualize and image what you want is a positive and effective tool toward change. It helps one to focus and it becomes a road map and guide to attainment. It is the ability to view your goal in your mind's eye and helps to keep you on track as you journey toward it.

It has been stated that imagery refers to "language that stimulates the reader's senses". It evokes the senses through taste, sound, smell, sight, and touch.

Today, I ask you to be aware of what you want to see for yourself in the future.

Do you see yourself:

Attaining a college degree.
Eating sensibly.
Securing that special job.
Learning to play an instrument or learning a new language.
Writing a book. etc.

This list is endless, it is personal to you. Some people use a vision board to keep the image fresh. Some write daily inspirations to keep it close to the surface.

Whatever or however you proceed, I urge you to use imagery, visualize the steps to follow and rejoice in its attainment.

FORGIVENESS

"To forgive is to set a prisoner free and discover that the prisoner was you."
—Lewis B. Smedes

Today's Thoughts for a Lifetime is Forgiveness. To be able to forgive is a statement only you can respond to. It means to pardon and end blame, to give absolution, vindicate, and to create self-compassion. This can be directed to the one who hurt you or the one you hurt, both are extremely important and necessary to move on in life. Today I ask you if that person you think you hurt is really YOU? Can you forgive yourself for experiencing something that ultimately caused you internal pain, self-doubt, and negativity?

To forgive yourself is a major challenge in life.

I have written about the importance of Loss in one's life and continue to believe that to make positive a sustainable change, one needs to acknowledge the loss, understand what it represents, and grieve it. Is this easy? No, it may feel insurmountable, but it is not. Believe in YOU! In that process, learn from your mistakes, take responsibility for your actions, turn guilt into gratitude and forgive yourself. Please be aware that Forgiveness is a process that leads to truth, belief, optimism, self-acceptance, and self-love. Mark Twain said, "Forgiveness is the fragrance that the violet sheds on the heel that has crushed it".

Forgiveness is a task and an action that requires one to understand, feel, and believe in and not let shame or guilt interfere with. It is a golden message that requires decision making and action to release it from your life. I believe it holds so much value and can be understood as another vehicle for positive change. Perhaps pontificate on it if you wish, **believe it, and allow the positivity of it to permeate your well-being.**

LISTENING

"Trees are the earth's endless effort to speak to the listening heaven."
—Rabindranath Tagore (d.1941)

Todays' Thoughts for a Lifetime includes tips and techniques about listening.

Listening is the key to effective communication. If we do not listen effectively, the message being communicated may well be misunderstood.

Do you pay attention during the listening process, perhaps by acknowledging what you heard? If so, this serves as confirmation for the parties involved.

Do you know that listening includes attitude, attention, and adjustment? Do you listen with care and openness, this adds clarity to the interaction? I believe this is paramount for the listening process to be understood. Do you open the lines of communication and listen before you attempt to make your point. The Bible says, "He who gives an answer before he hears, it is folly and shame to him".
—Proverb 18:13

When you are listening, you can eliminate mixed messages. I personally feel very uncomfortable and confused by mixed messages.

Are you aware of your mood when listening, this could help with the result of the communication?

Do you know that when the conversation ends, it is always a good idea to briefly review what transpired? This gives closure. This paves the way to future interaction when needed.

REMEMBER: Part of being successful in life is to question and listen. I hope you find the above Tip of the Day to be helpful and thought provoking.

LIFE IS A BOWL OF CHERRIES

Last night I found myself humming a tune that I could not recollect. As I listened to myself clues and memories, as a very young child, listening to my mother sing began to surface, but what was it? 'POP' in a flash I remembered the song, it is Life Is Just a Bowl Of Cherries. Yes, a very, very, old tune. Maybe I am dating myself but obviously that tune stayed with me. The phrase, life is like a bowl of cherries, was common to many and has been around for decades, some say it began during the Great Depression, yet others believe it was earlier.

The expression that life is like a bowl of cherries represents the unpredictability of life, sometimes it's like cherries, sweet, or sour or even rotten, all possibilities in life.

I understand that in "days of old", bowls of cherries were common on many tables in restaurants and in homes. This was connected to family, friends, communication and other such gatherings. It had an enormous cultural impact. The words focus on positivity, appreciation and letting go of worrying and other such stressors. It calls attention to the unpredictability of life, from sweet to sour and back.

Life serves up sweet moments, like those of sweet cherries. Life also serves up those unexpected sour moments that catch us off guard. We must embrace both. We cannot control every flavor, but we can choose how we react and what we do at the time.

Today's Thought for a Lifetime is to remind us to believe, and sing the message that life is like a bowl of cherries. It is unpredictable, yes, but it fosters resiliency and the flavors of life. One message in the 1930's song by Lew Brown and Ray Henderson suggests "to live and laugh at it all". What do you think and believe?

ALERT-THE HOLIDAY SEASON IS NEAR

As I look around and realize how close the holidays are, I think of the issue of food, presents, family and much more. Many of the people I have spoken to in my lifetime personally and professionally have mixed emotions around this time. Some of the points I'd like to make are the following. Please know this is an extremely short list, but hopefully a helpful one.

Enjoy your holiday!
How Should I Eat?
First, Begin to Plan Ahead.
Eliminate Stressful Events=Stressful Eating.
Plan to enjoy the holiday-make it filled with the meaning of it.
Allow yourself to eat with comfort & care.
Practice Modification-No Stuffing but eat, do not starve or deny.
Don't sit at the dinner table for hours.
Reframe negativity to positivity.
Enjoy the company.
Be grateful for its meaning & gifts of life.
Allow yourself to enjoy it.

My core message for today's Thought for a Lifetime is Live, Enjoy, Count Your Blessings, Communicate and be Grateful for YOU and Who You Are!

THE VALUE OF VALUE

"Know the true value of time, snatch, seize, and enjoy every moment of it. No idleness, no laziness, no procrastination, never put off till tomorrow what you can do today."

—Philip Stanhope, 4th Earl of Chesterfield

Today's Thoughts for a Lifetime is the Value of Value, which has many connections, meanings, and values to each of us. My contribution to the impending New Year is to ask you to ponder what Value means to you, its purpose, and its connection to your sense of self and life. Questions I find myself thinking about are:

What do I value in Life?
How do I value myself and my inspirations in life?
Do I undervalue or overvalue both myself or that which I experience or
    think I want to Experience.

The meaning of self-value has roots in whether you believe you are worthy of respect, love, and well-being. Self-value is not self-absorption or selfishness, it is the act of cultivating self-respect, within healthy boundaries for the self and others in your life. This subject is connected to various forms of one's sense of self.

The purpose of this Thoughts for a Lifetime is to whet the appetite and encourage one's understanding of this topic. It is to open one's eyes, thoughts, and beliefs about this subject as it relates to your past, but more importantly how it relates to your future.

Today I encourage you to explore the Value of Value in your life. I sincerely wish and send you encouragement and belief in your future as we enter the year 2023. Love to all, and to your life which is truly precious.

"Life is not about finding yourself. Life is about creating yourself."
—George Bernard Shaw

TO BE LISTENED TO

"Temperance – There is no difference between knowledge and temperance; for he who knows what is good and embraces it, who knows what is bad and avoids it is learned and temperate."
—Socrates

Recently a patient came into my office very upset with herself. Her brother who suffered from advanced dementia would have periodic episodes of agitation. Although she understood him and was very caring, she noticed her response to him on several occasions was short-tempered. She accepted and loved him and was always trying to please him, however on a day in which he TOTALLY refused to put a halt to his behavior, an anger permeated her soul with an indescribable force. She was able to calm herself but not without question and guilt. She experienced an "emotional pain", and doubt as a "good person." This left her with an indescribable feeling. Was she "a bad person" she questioned; the guilt seemed inconsolable. "I do not understand where this is coming from". This was the theme of our session.

What was the outcome, you might question. The issue of <u>not being listened to and heard </u>was the driving force behind her reaction. A light bulb in her mind brightened with this self-realization and the ongoing exploration that followed.

Today's Thoughts for a Lifetime is Not Being Listened To and Heard. I began to think of myself and one's self-perspective to such situations in life. I reflected on my work with so many patients who worked on the same theme in treatment. What thoughts, feelings, beliefs, and actions surface? These and other questions help us to understand ourselves. Once we define what they are, it opens the door to more awareness, self-acceptance, courage, and faith in ourselves.

Please reflect on the above, what is stirring inside you as you ponder this?

Shakespeare stated, "There's nothing either good or bad, but thinking makes it so."

TREASURE CHEST

"Guard well within yourself that treasure, kindness, know how to give without hesitation, how to lose without regret, how to acquire without meanness.".
—George Sand

My Thoughts for a Lifetime today calls attention to the following question. Do you have a treasure chest, what is in it, what do you want to put in it?

What defines a treasure? It could be something we appreciate, value, and love. It could be wealth of any kind, jewelry, money, and other riches. The one on the top of my list is the value of people esteemed as rare and precious to me, friendships, family, plus the memories that I cherish.

My treasure chest holds many if not all the above. Sometimes we tend to take those treasures for grant it or forget about them. Life often becomes busier than we wish, sometimes leading us to focus on the negative vs. what is positive.

Do you value the treasures within you? If you have a treasure chest, have you looked at what is in it and/or have you added anything to it? It is the holder of a lifetime of memories of any kind. It holds memories of what was, what is and perhaps what will be.

If your treasure chest has been in the attic, move it, open it, review, and value it as you begin to add to it. Do not tarnish the gift of memory and your mind, rather acknowledge, and enhance it.

"Memory Is the treasure house of the mind wherein the monuments thereof are kept and preserved."
—Thomas Fuller

THE PRESENT

"As long as you live keep learning how to live."
—Lucius Annaeus Seneca (65AD)

Today's Thoughts for a Lifetime is The Present.

Here it is 11:28AM, I have been up since 7AM. My goal and enthusiasm were to continue writing. After publishing Parting Is Such Sweet Sorrow. Saying goodbye to an eating problem, the realization to add to it soon followed. Thoughts of a workbook with exercises, treatment suggestions and motivational tidbits danced in my head. Yet, as I sit here my mind seems to be floating to multiple places with a plethora of thoughts, yet none of them are complete.

Plato stated," the beginning is the most important part of the work", but I am having difficulty getting started. So, what is the problem? I asked myself, is it this, that, or another thing? The light bulb brightens, I am not present or focused mentally and probably emotionally as well. Although the reasons could be many. I recalled Spencer Johnson's book titled The Present. I truly believe that it is a Present we give ourselves to be Present. At this time, I feel elated that my recall trickled into my confused mind. I remembered that Johnson explored the following, which I want to share with those who may be reading this TFL.

To look at what is right and stay focused. Ask yourself what is important for you today.

To look at the past and learn from it. To recall past situations and learn from them to do things differently.

To see how you can create a future. Specifically, when you want to improve your future.

To see the value of purpose. Learn to make your life and work more meaningful.

The fireworks in my mind began to explode, I was on my way. I thought to myself:

This TFL was something I wanted to do, I needed to focus on it right now.

Thoughts for a Lifetime

Put on the music I love; this motivates my heart and soul.
Sit back and relax, release the pressure which is self-inflicted and accept
  this Present.
Value my decision to write, allow the peace I feel to permeate within.

Isaac Newton said. "My powers are ordinary, only my application brings
me success". If you wish, reflect on the above perhaps you will give yourself a
Present, just as I have.

APPRECIATION AND SORROW

Appreciation. "One of the Godlike things in this world is the veneration done to human worth by the hearts of men."
—Carlyle

As I walked outside today, my breath skipped a beat, it was so cold that my face and hands felt frozen within minutes.

However, with each step, I felt invigorated. The sight of snow and the scent of fresh air made up for the initial semi-shock of the cold. In the distance I saw deer who were enjoying the snow. There were no birds chirping or leaves blowing and the silence I experienced was a source of calm as I journeyed down my path. My senses of sight, smell, hearing, and feeling were awoken. Winter is a season that many people I know tend to hibernate, thankfully I feel very different about that, today was an example of that for me.

Today was reminiscent of my childhood and the childhood of my children. Oh, how we all loved the snow and the brisk feeling experienced. Was it cold, were we tired and wet from frolicking in the snow? Yes. But those were memories I still cherish.

Today's TFL may sound soapy, however I like soapy sometimes. Perhaps there are times that you reflect on moments that sound like mine.

Life creates bundles of memories. Some are sorrowful, yet some are appreciated, enjoyed, and cherished.

My message is to stay focused and recognize that when one door closes another one DOES open. Integrate this thought and make it yours.

Ponder this message and ask yourself! "Is there more appreciation in your heart than sorrow in your heart"?

Make it so, believe it, breath in the crisp feel of the air and follow its message.

LOVE AND RELATIONSHIP

"Where there is love there is life."
　　　　　　　　　　　　　—Mahatma Gandhi

Today's Thoughts for a Lifetime is a reflection on true love. There are many definitions and examples of true love. What follows is the summary of a story I read in the June 2009 Psychospiritual Therapy newsletter. This story is special, it is titled: <u>How to Dance in the Rain.</u>

David Wilkerson wrote "Love is not only something you feel, but also something you do". Below is a summary of this article as I understand it.

An elderly man arrived at a medical clinic to have stitches removed as a result of a minor injury. He was concerned finding out that the wait would be over an hour. The nurse questioned his apparent time concern. He replied that he had to meet his wife for breakfast who was in a nursing home. Upon asking about his wife's health, he informed her that she had advanced Alzheimer's Disease and no longer recognized him for over 5 years. This surprised the nurse who gently questioned why he continued to go even though she no longer recognized him. He lovingly replied that although she doesn't know him however he still knew her.

With tears in her eyes, the nurse thought that this is the kind of love she wanted in her life.

True love is neither physical, nor romantic. True love is an acceptance of all that is, has been, will be and will not be. "Life isn't about how to survive the storm, but how to dance in the rain." I am emotionally touched each time I read this story.

The above TFL reflects aspects of a successful relationship. Love can be defined in many ways but openness, empathy, loyalty, respect and trust are among the definitions of true love.

What do you think?

SHADOWS OF A TREASURE

"For Where Your Treasure Is, There Also Will Your Heart Be"
—Matthew 6:21

While driving I looked over to the passenger seat. Today my husband of 54 years was home but there are times he is sitting there. Today I reflect on how this strong minded man, who worked hard all his life, is a shadow of who he was. His beliefs and ethics were something we shared. Were there times when we didn't see eye to eye? Yes. If that was not the case one could say that my perception was not realistic or that I was in a world of denial. However, we were partners who could appreciate and trust each other.

The pain I feel today is nothing new. It is shared with so many memories. What are they you ask? They are my ability to care for him, care for myself and family and attempt to care for mankind in my own way. Is that how you always feel you ask? No, but that is how I see life. Wanting to do and be, just as he would want for me and for himself if this was reversed.

I want to capture and hold the shadows of my life and the shadow of this man who he was, who he is today and will be. I have realized so much during this journey. My treasures have been many, but he is my treasure, and this is where my heart will always be. Thank you! (Year 2021)

THE MASTER OF YOUR DESTINY

"One's destination is never a place but rather a new way of looking at things."
—Henry Miller

The concept of being the Master of your Destiny crept into my mind recently. Perhaps it had to do with situations I did or did not think I had control of. Perhaps it had to do with the realization that life passes relatively quickly. If that is the case, how do we view it and believe that it can be.

The Free Dictionary states the Master of Your Destiny is "one who makes one's own decisions about or directly controls the course of one's future, independent of the desires, expectations, or machinations of others." The concepts of imagery, positive thinking, mind control, belief systems, began to spin in my head like a storm about to begin. "But wait" I said to myself, let me not rush into a plethora of thoughts, but rather examine them one at a time.

What am I thinking and can I put these into practice. Do I want to make changes? Do I want to see where the journey leads me? These and many other questions will likely exist within my mind, often before I decide to move into action. Apprehension, confusion, hesitation, are part of the doubts I experience. The opposite of doubt or uncertainty is peace, calm, and belief.

Regardless of what I chose to do, the reality is that I am the Master of My Destiny. That explanation and meaning can have a newfound effect on my sense of being and belief. Do I believe in myself and the ability to work toward and accept that belief? Today's Thought for a Lifetime is DO YOU BELIEVE YOU ARE THE MASTER OF YOUR DESTINY?

The Book of Revelation states: "Your destiny is to fulfill those things upon which you focus most intently. So, choose to keep your focus on that which is truly magnificent, beautiful, uplifting, and joyful. Your life is always moving toward something." Ralph Martson

THE JOURNEY

"A log is floating down a river, on one bank is indulgence, and on the other is deprivation. As the log flows down the river, it passes both extremes. If it gets stuck on either extreme, the log sinks or rots. But when it follows the middle path, it floats down the river and reaches the ocean of freedom"
—The Zen of Eating, Kabatznick

The above quote can apply to many things in life. In my mind it represents all or nothing thinking. This can be representative in relationships, eating, drinking, purchasing, and attitudes about anything. Balance or taking the middle path is positive and worth it on many levels, try it.

Look at your mental attitude to see what the struggle is and identify your reactions.

Stay on the course, follow the middle path, and see how you think and feel.

Good Luck on the Journey!

TO BELIEVE

"We all have the power to make wishes come true as long as we keep believing".
—Louisa May Alcott

Today's Thoughts for a Lifetime is To Believe.

If only we could believe in the beauty of life.
If only we could believe that because life has its twists and turns, change is possible.
If only we believe that after the hurricanes of life comes peace.
If only we could scream from the highest mountain that life is good if we are grateful for what we are given.
If only we could believe that we could plant the seeds and from those seeds will grow beauty, peace, and love.
If only we could believe that weeds can be picked and discarded.
If only we could believe in the power of fun, joy, and laughter.
If only we could believe that music can sooth the soul.
If only we could believe in ourselves.
LET US BELIEVE!

THE MORAL OF THE STORY

Recently I came across a bit of inspiration that touched me once again. You see the story I revisited was one I had saved as an inspiration to be used with those who needed it or for future writings I intended to do someday. The body of the story had to do with the kindness of people. This was one story of many we hear about in books, movies, conversations, and life. Today the Thoughts for a Lifetime is not the story but the moral of the story, which is that we will not be remembered by our words, but by your kind deeds. It has been noted it is not measured by the breaths we take, rather by the moments that take our breath.

"It's not what you gather, but what you scatter that tells what kind of life you have lived."

The question today is: What takes your breath?

> During the fall we see the leaves turning multiple colors and falling. The bed of color is amazing.
> During the winter a brisk walk, breathing in the air we take in. Perhaps snow dusts the walkways, reminding us of the beauty of nature and impending holidays.
> During the spring when the sound of birds who feel free and safe fly overhead.
> During the summer when the sun shines. After a walk outside when the grass is cut along with the scent of blossoming flowers is indescribable. There is a sense of renewal and growth.
> The beauty of a new baby cooing and growing.
> When graduating or attaining that special job.
> How we feel when we help another and the feeling of humility and gratitude when we are helped by another.
> To have meaning and purpose in life.
> These and so much more are a pinhole of life that can take our breath.
> Sit back, take in the beauty of life, share with loved ones, for that is what we can share.

Louise Parente

"There is a destiny that makes us brothers. None goes his way alone. All that we send into the lives of others comes back into our own."
—Markham

THE GIFTS AND TREASURES OF LIFE

"Nature is man's teacher. She unfolds her treasures to his search, unseals his eye, illumes his mind, and purifies his heart; an influence breathes from all the sights and sounds of her existence."
—Street

Today I am putting the finishing touches in my future book, Thoughts for a Lifetime. Meaningful Nuggets of Life. In doing so the desire to write another TFL propelled me to write about the gifts and treasures of life.

The gifts of life often refer to the opportunity to live, experience and learn. The treasures of life often refer to the simple, meaningful experiences and relationships that led to joy, fulfillment and connection. The importance of our emotions and true inner thoughts and feelings are needed to explore, time, talent, treasure, love and life. These are the gifts and treasures to be grateful for. The balance of emotions leads to the ability to cope with life's ups and downs thus enhancing a life to be lived more fully and authentically. The realization that the gifts and treasures in life are within is my message today.

"THE SEARCH – If you ever find happiness by hunting for it, you will find it as the old woman did her lost spectacles, safe on her own nose all the time."
—Jos Billings

Thanks for Listening!

FINAL THOUGHTS

As I write this final section of *Thoughts for a Lifetime-Meaningful Nuggets of Life*, I find my mind whirling with so many feelings and thoughts. I hope that anyone who reads these thoughts will find them to be valuable, helpful and heartfelt.

My desire to continue to create and add future Thoughts for a Lifetime have never stopped, thus I have and will continue to do so.

I encourage you, my readers to be the Master of your Destiny, and continue to add to the repertoire of your life while being grateful for it.

With appreciation in my heart, I remain,

—Louise Parente

BIBLIOGRAPHY

Johnson, Spencer. The Present: The Gift for Changing time. Crown Currency Publishing, 2010.

Kabctznick, Ronna. The Zen of Eating. R.A.Katnik, 1998.

Lazarus, Arnold. The Practice of Multimodal Therapy. Systematic And Effective Psychotherapy. Maryland: Johns Hopkins University Press, 1989.

Lytle, Clyde Francis, Ed. Leaves of Gold, An Anthology of Prayers, Memorable Phrases, Inspirational Verse and Prose. Pennsylvania: Collette Publishing, 1964.

Parente, Louise. Parting is Such Sweet Sorrow. Saying Goodbye to an Eating Problem. Indiana: Balboa Press Publishing, 2020.

Parente, Louise. Changing Your Relationship with Food Once and for All: The Ultimate Workbook. New Jersey: Appreciation Publishing, 2024.

Psychospiritual Therapy Newsletter, June 2009.

Ruiz, Don Miguel. The Four Agreements. California: Amber-Allen Publishing, 1997.